# Application Delivery and Load Balancing in Microsoft Azure

*Practical Solutions with NGINX and Microsoft Azure*

*Derek DeJonghe and Arlan Nugara*

Beijing · Boston · Farnham · Sebastopol · Tokyo

**Application Delivery and Load Balancing in Microsoft Azure**

by Derek DeJonghe and Arlan Nugara

Published by O'Reilly Media, Inc., 1005 Gravenstein Highway North, Sebastopol, CA 95472.

O'Reilly books may be purchased for educational, business, or sales promotional use. Online editions are also available for most titles (*https://oreilly.com*). For more information, contact our corporate/institu-tional sales department: 800-998-9938 or *corporate@oreilly.com*.

**Acquisitions Editor:** Mary Preap
**Development Editor:** Gary O'Brien
**Production Editor:** Daniel Elfanbaum
**Copyeditor:** Arthur Johnson
**Proofreader:** Piper Editorial LLC

**Indexer:** Judith McConville
**Interior Designer:** David Futato
**Cover Designer:** Karen Montgomery
**Illustrator:** Kate Dullea

December 2020:     First Edition

**Revision History for the First Edition**
2020-12-04:    First Release

See *https://oreilly.com/catalog/errata.csp?isbn=9781098115869* for release details.

978-1-098-11586-9

[LSI]

# Table of Contents

# Preface

This book is intended for cloud solution architects and software architects looking to distribute load across multiple servers, applications, or regions within Microsoft Azure. Load balancing is used to improve performance and availability; however, the layer that is used to perform the load balancing action has evolved to become much more. This layer of a web application stack is known as the data plane, and it is used to transmit requests and connections to an application. The data plane can be used to validate, route, and manipulate inbound communication from clients to an application. By building up your control of this layer, you can optimize and facilitate your exact use case.

Throughout this book you will learn how load balancing and the data plane can be integral facets of your application delivery. We will discuss load balancing and application delivery in general before moving on to inform you about the available native options within Azure and explaining the software-based data plane solution known as NGINX (pronounced "engine-ex"), which can be used independently of your infrastructure provider. We will then discuss integrating NGINX with Azure and how native Azure services paired with NGINX can be complementary.

Once we have an understanding of the load-balancing data plane options available to us, we'll detail governance and monitoring of a given solution within Azure. Regarding this topic, we'll introduce the NGINX platform solution for control and configuration known as NGINX Controller. Finally, we'll wrap up with a section about security and how we can enable our data plane to be an invaluable asset in security and threat management.

While the examples and context will be specific to Microsoft Azure, the methodologies and overarching concepts will hold true for any cloud or infrastructure provider. It is our hope that those ideas impact you the most and enable you to design and implement secure, highly scalable, and highly available solutions.

# Conventions Used in This Book

The following typographical conventions are used in this book:

*Italic*
> Indicates new terms, URLs, email addresses, filenames, and file extensions.

`Constant width`
> Used for program listings, as well as within paragraphs to refer to program elements such as variable or function names, databases, data types, environment variables, statements, and keywords.

**`Constant width bold`**
> Shows commands or other text that should be typed literally by the user.

 This element signifies a tip or suggestion.

 This element signifies a general note.

 This element indicates a warning or caution.

# Using Code Examples

If you have a technical question or a problem using the code examples, please send an email to *bookquestions@oreilly.com*.

This book is here to help you get your job done. In general, if example code is offered with this book, you may use it in your programs and documentation. You do not need to contact us for permission unless you're reproducing a significant portion of the code. For example, writing a program that uses several chunks of code from this book does not require permission. Selling or distributing examples from O'Reilly books does require permission. Answering a question by citing this book and quoting example code does not require permission. Incorporating a significant amount of example code from this book into your product's documentation does require permission.

We appreciate, but generally do not require, attribution. An attribution usually includes the title, author, publisher, and ISBN. For example: "*Application Delivery and Load Balancing in Microsoft Azure* by Derek DeJonghe and Arlan Nugara (O'Reilly). Copyright 2021 O'Reilly Media, 978-1-098-11586-9."

If you feel your use of code examples falls outside fair use or the permission given above, feel free to contact us at *permissions@oreilly.com*.

## O'Reilly Online Learning

 For more than 40 years, *O'Reilly Media* has provided technology and business training, knowledge, and insight to help companies succeed.

Our unique network of experts and innovators share their knowledge and expertise through books, articles, and our online learning platform. O'Reilly's online learning platform gives you on-demand access to live training courses, in-depth learning paths, interactive coding environments, and a vast collection of text and video from O'Reilly and 200+ other publishers. For more information, visit *http://oreilly.com*.

## How to Contact Us

Please address comments and questions concerning this book to the publisher:

O'Reilly Media, Inc.
1005 Gravenstein Highway North
Sebastopol, CA 95472
800-998-9938 (in the United States or Canada)
707-829-0515 (international or local)
707-829-0104 (fax)

We have a web page for this book, where we list errata, examples, and any additional information. You can access this page at *https://oreil.ly/adlbma*.

Email *bookquestions@oreilly.com* to comment or ask technical questions about this book. For news and information about our books and courses, visit *http://oreilly.com*.

Find us on Facebook: *http://facebook.com/oreilly*

Follow us on Twitter: *http://twitter.com/oreillymedia*

Watch us on YouTube: *http://youtube.com/oreillymedia*

# Acknowledgments

We would like to thank our technical reviewers Shahid Iqbal, Deepak Kaushik, Daniel Patrick, and Ryan Tasson for their efforts and valuable feedback. Being able to balance the work of authoring and producing this title has made possible its delivery to you, our readers.

# CHAPTER 1

# What Are Application Delivery and Load Balancing, and Why Are They Important?

When anyone uses an application, they expect it to respond quickly, efficiently, and reliably. When a user encounters errors, outages, or overcapacity messages, they generally don't wonder why. They get annoyed, quit using the application, and ultimately complain about the application's owner on social media. It doesn't matter that the company was having a great day, and that requests to their servers went through the roof. What matters is that the user's request resulted in a failure of the application and, in the user's eyes, the company providing the application.

As more companies move their applications and services to the cloud, responding to variable demands and workloads has become increasingly important. In this chapter, we'll introduce the concepts behind application delivery and load balancing by explaining the purpose of application delivery controllers and load balancers and the problems they solve. Subsequent chapters will explore how you can use Microsoft Azure and NGINX for high-performance application delivery and load balancing.

## Application Delivery Controllers

Put simply, application delivery is a process that ensures that an application is delivered properly and efficiently to its clients, no matter the load or the behind-the-scenes process and availability. Servers can fail for any number of reasons, from demand capacity to security breaches or a simple mechanical failure. When that server is solely responsible for delivery of an application that customers or employees are relying on, then the application also fails. Organizations need ways to be adaptable and provide optimal performance and availability in any given situation.

At the heart of modern web application delivery is a data plane, which makes possible the application's delivery to the client. Modern data planes are typically made up of reverse proxies working together to provide an optimal experience to the user. An advanced proxy with routing, authentication, and security controls is often referred to as an application delivery controller (ADC). ADCs help ensure maximum performance and capacity by sitting between the user and the application servers, directing valid requests only to servers that are currently online. Thus, an ADC offers a layer of control between the user experience and the application.

## Hardware or Software

All ADCs are essentially software solutions that receive a network transmission and elevate it to the application layer for full control. On-premises hardware/software bundled black-box options are available for purchase from vendors. However, the hardware is not the special sauce; it's the software the machine runs that provides you the control over your application's delivery. In today's world, disruptors are those who are able to move quickly and adapt to changes in technology, which leaves no room for lengthy hardware procurement and installation processes.

If an ADC vendor does not have a virtual appliance or software solution available, then you need to reconsider your vendor. Hardware optimization and acceleration makes a minimal impact on business value compared to agility.

## Structure and Function of ADCs

In general, an ADC accepts a request from a client and decides how best to serve that specific request based on rules in its configuration. An ADC may receive a request, validate its intended route and method, pass it through processing for security vulnerabilities, validate its authentication and authorization, and manipulate headers or the like before making a request on behalf of the client to an application server (one that the ADC knows is responsive) to fulfill the request.

This process may happen at multiple layers within a web application's stack. An ADC that is positioned in close proximity to a client may proxy the request to an ADC that is in closer proximity to the application servers. Both ADCs enable control of how your application is delivered to the client, at different levels, to provide you maximum configurability.

An ADC may be in place for a specific application or accept requests for a number of purposes to solve the needs of your use case. At their core, ADCs are proxies configured as necessary to deliver your application.

# Load Balancers

Optimal load distribution reduces site inaccessibility caused by failure or stress of a single server while assuring consistent performance for all users. Different routing techniques and algorithms ensure optimal performance in varying load-balancing scenarios.

Modern websites must support concurrent connections from clients requesting text, images, video, or application data, all in a fast and reliable manner, while scaling from hundreds of users to millions of users during peak times. Load balancers are a critical part of this scalability.

Load balancers, introduced in the 1990s as hardware-based servers or appliances, have evolved considerably. Managed cloud load balancing is an updated alternative to hardware load balancers; they provide a configuration interface, but you don't have to manage hardware, software, updates, or anything but the configuration. Regardless of the implementation of a load balancer, scalability is still the primary goal of load balancing, even though modern load balancers can do so much more. Figure 1-1 shows a basic load-balancing solution. The client in any of these scenarios might be an end user's browser, a mobile application, or another web service.

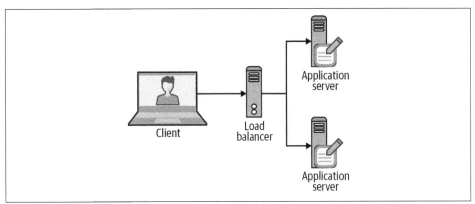

*Figure 1-1. Diagram of a basic load-balancing solution.*

An ADC will perform load balancing when multiple possible responders are configured for a given request. Many ADCs will enable configuration of the algorithm that it uses to select which responder it proxies a given request to, which in turn is how it balances load.

## The OSI Model and Load Balancing

Before we discuss load balancing, especially in the cloud, in any more detail, it's important to review the Open System Interconnection (OSI) model. This conceptual model provides a visual representation of the interoperation between systems that is universally applicable no matter what hardware or network characteristics are involved. The OSI model performs no functions in the networking process. It is a conceptual framework to help understand complex interactions. The model defines a networking framework that implements seven layers:

- Layer 7: Application layer
- Layer 6: Presentation layer
- Layer 5: Session layer
- Layer 4: Transport layer
- Layer 3: Network layer
- Layer 2: Data-link layer
- Layer 1: Physical layer

Network firewalls are security devices that operate from Layer 1 to Layer 3, whereas load balancing happens at Layer 4 and Layer 7. Load balancers have different capabilities, including the following:

*Layer 4 (L4)*
    Directs traffic based on data from network and transport layer protocols, such as IP address and TCP port.

*Layer 7 (L7)*
    Adds context switching to load balancing, allowing routing decisions based on attributes like HTTP header, URL, Secure Sockets Layer (SSL) session ID, and HTML form data.

*Global Server Load Balancing (GSLB)*
    Extends L4 and L7 capabilities to servers in different geographic locations. The Domain Name System (DNS) is also used in certain solutions, and this topic is addressedm when Azure Traffic Manager is used as an example of such an implementation.

Demand for more control over the configurability of load balancers and the data plane in general is increasing dramatically as the capabilities become more apparent to more organizations. This demand drives innovation in technology, which has given birth to the world of ADCs.

## Problems Load Balancers Solve

Load balancing solves for capacity and availability but also gives way for scalability. These concepts hold true at local and global levels. By balancing load at different layers, we're able to direct client requests across multiple application servers, between multiple data centers, and over groups of data centers in different regions of the world.

Imagine—or maybe you don't have to—that your application needs to be performant to users worldwide, which means that it needs to be hosted in multiple geographically separated locations. You use global load balancing to direct a client request to the least latent physical entity representing your application. For availability's sake, that geographical location is made up of multiple data centers. You use load balancing to distribute loads between those data centers. For capacity's sake, you have multiple servers within a data center that are able to respond to a given request; if the load for a data center within the geographical location is too much for a single server to handle, you'd then load balance over those different servers.

In this scenario, we have three layers of load balancers to deliver a single globally scalable application. When a server is at peak capacity within a data center, there's another server to help out. If a data center is at peak capacity or in failure, you have another data center to handle the load. In the case of an entire geographical location being out of service or at peak capacity, the load balancer makes the decision to route the request to another location. No matter the level your application is struggling at, your client's request will still be fulfilled.

## The Solutions Load Balancers Provide

The number of layers of load balancing depends on the needs of your application. How a load balancer determines where to direct a request is based on its own algorithm. The algorithms provided by a load balancer depend on the solution; however, most have a common set to fit your application and client needs:

*Round robin*
> The default load-balancing solution, in which requests are distributed through the list of servers sequentially.

*Weighted round robin*
> Round robin for situations in which the capacities of the servers vary. The servers with the higher weight are favored and receive a greater share of the traffic.

*Weighted least connections*
> Similar to round robin, weighted least connections gives a weighted status to each server; the load balancer routes traffic based on the least number of open connections.

*Hashing*
> An algorithm generates a hash key from the header or other information to direct traffic to a specific server.

Other than load distribution, a load balancer can enforce session persistence, also referred to as a sticky session. This involves directing incoming client requests to the same backend server for the duration of a client session. This is a solution to a problem that load balancing presents. A backend server may store data locally for a number of reasons—if, for example, the data set is too large to work with over the network in a timely fashion. In this event, the client will want subsequent requests to be directed to the same backend server—hence session persistence. If a client request is directed to a server that does not have access to the session state data, the client may be logged out or see inconsistent results between requests.

A key feature of load balancers is to monitor the health of a server and to ensure that client requests are not directed to a backend server that is unavailable or unhealthy. A load balancer will either actively or passively monitor its backend servers and can mark them as unhealthy under certain conditions.

## Application Delivery and Load Balancing: A Solution Overview

Load balancing and application delivery are interrelated solutions. To understand their relationship and how load balancing is key to application delivery, let's quickly review the delivery process without an ADC or load balancing:

1. An end user/client makes a request to connect with an application on a server. The request is routed over the internet to the application server.
2. The server accepts the connection and responds.
3. The user/client receives the response to their request.

Figure 1-2 illustrates this process. From the user/client perspective, this was a direct connection. The user asked the application to do something, and it responded.

In an application delivery environment, an ADC sits somewhere between the user/client and the virtual application servers where the requested service resides. The delivery process would look something like the following:

1. An end user/client makes a request to connect with an application on a server. The request is routed over the internet to the ADC.
2. The ADC decides to accept the connection and then matches the request with the appropriate destination.
3. The ADC makes a request to the designated application server.
4. The application server responds to the ADC.
5. The user/client receives the response to their request.

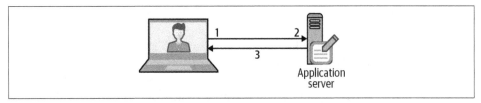

*Figure 1-2. Diagram of basic application delivery transaction solution.*

Figure 1-3 shows the application delivery process with an ADC. From the user/client perspective, this was a direct connection. They would have no indication that any action took place between them and the application. During the transaction, the ADC determines the appropriate application endpoint to respond to the client's request. The diagram depicts the request being directed to Application A.

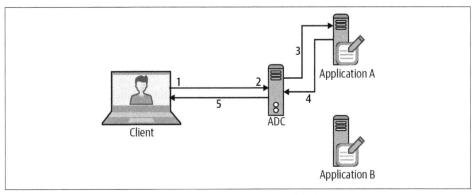

*Figure 1-3. Diagram of application delivery with a load-balancing ADC.*

In general, an ADC sits between a client and a server. It does not matter whether the client is a user, a web application/service, or another ADC. In the eyes of an ADC, the connection being received is a client of the ADC, and its job is to handle each request according to its configuration.

In regard to redundancy and scale, an ADC is able to balance load over sets of virtual servers that are grouped by application. By combining the routing and control functionality of an ADC with load balancing, we are able to reduce the number of hops a request must take through different layers and services, which in turn optimizes network performance while optimizing availability, reliability, and application responsiveness.

# Conclusion

While basic load balancing is still widely used, many web application teams are starting to see their load balancing layer as the prime point at which to add more functionality. Such functionality includes Layer 7 request routing, request and authorization validation, as well as other features that will be covered in this book. The heart of application delivery is the ADC, an advanced load balancer that receives requests and directs them to servers to optimize performance and capacity, just as the heart delivers blood to the body's organs. Without load balancing, most modern applications would fail. It's not enough to simply make an application reachable; it also must be dependable, functional, and, most importantly, always available.

As companies move applications from on-premises to the cloud, software architects and cloud solution architects are looking at options to improve application delivery, load balancing, performance, security, and high availability for workloads. This book will provide a meaningful description of application delivery and load-balancing options available natively from Microsoft Azure and of the role NGINX can provide in a comprehensive solution.

In Chapter 2, we'll explore the managed solutions that are available in Azure, including its native load balancers, application gateway, web application firewalls, and Azure Front Door.

# Managed Load-Balancing Options in Azure

Microsoft Azure, like other cloud service providers, offers the ability to instantly provision computing resources on demand. This includes support for fully managed Azure services such as load balancers, as well as support for third-party network virtual appliance load balancers such as NGINX. There are four native managed load-balancing services in Azure to ensure always-available applications both on the public internet and on private or virtual networks. This chapter will explore the features and capabilities of these four services to show how to improve load balancing, performance, security, and high availability for workloads on Azure. Each solution has its own pricing model; for the most part, the pricing calculation is based on request count and amount of data processed, although Azure Application Gateway does have a base cost associated with its usage per hour.

## Azure Native Load Balancing

The Azure managed services that provide load balancing functionality enable load balancing in different ways and at different layers of the stack. These services complement one another and can be layered to provide the intended type of service.

- Azure Load Balancer is a Layer 4 (transport layer) service that handles UDP and TCP protocols.

- Azure Application Gateway is a Layer 7 HTTP load balancer with an application delivery controller and SSL/TLS termination offload capabilities.

- Azure Traffic Manager provides DNS-based, domain-level load balancing.

- Azure Front Door is a full Layer 7 application delivery network with extensive features, positioned to optimize for network latency and proximity.

We'll review each service to understand when to use it effectively. First though, it's important to understand Azure's load-balancing dimensions.

## Azure Load-Balancing Dimensions

Azure breaks out its load-balancing services along two dimensions: global or regional, and HTTP(S) or non-HTTP(S). Each of these dimensions, or any combination thereof, offers different solutions based on business needs. Table 2-1 shows where each Azure Load Balancer falls among the dimensions.

*Table 2-1. Azure load balancers by dimension*

| Load balancing service | Global or regional | Traffic type | OSI layer |
| --- | --- | --- | --- |
| Azure Load Balancer | Regional | Non-HTTP(S) | Layer 4 |
| Azure Application Gateway | Regional | HTTP(S) | Layer 7 |
| Azure Front Door | Global | HTTP(S) | Layer 7 |
| Azure Traffic Manager | Global | Non-HTTP(S) | Layer 7 |

### Global versus regional load balancing

A global load balancer efficiently distributes traffic across distributed server clusters, including localized or regional backends, multiple data centers, public or private clouds, and hybrid/on-premises, no matter their location globally. Traffic is first routed to the closest available location to reduce latency and increase performance and availability. If the closest available location is unavailable or unreliable, the load balancer will move to the next closest one, and so on. Globalized load balancing also allows for serving localized content based on the request's originating IP address, to meet GDPR (General Data Protection Regulation) compliance, for example.

Regional load balancing distributes traffic across virtual machines in a virtual network or when all your servers are in a single region.

### HTTP(S) versus Non-HTTP(S)

These terms for describing the traffic type, HTTP(S) and non-HTTP(S), are used by Azure. HTTP(S) load-balancing services operate on Layer 7, the application layer, and only accept HTTP(S) traffic for web applications or other HTTP(S) destinations. They include features such as SSL offload, web application firewalls, and path-based and domain (host header)-based routing. Non-HTTP(S) load-balancing services have a broader scope than HTTP(S) services, as they operate lower in the OSI model, supporting TCP and UDP.

Now that we understand Azure's approach to load balancing, we'll walk through the purpose, use, and features of all four load-balancing services.

### Load Balancer decision diagram

Figure 2-1 is a diagram to help explain which combination of Azure managed offer-ings is useful for a given scenario. For example, assume you have a public-facing HTTP(S) application that is deployed to multiple Azure regions and that follows a microservice architecture. You would follow the diagram, answering the first ques-tion—yes, the application is HTTP(S)—and then the next question—yes, the applica-tion is internet facing. With a microservice architecture, it's likely that you may need application-layer processing, or routing. In this scenario, you would follow the dia-gram to the Azure Front Door + Application Gateway solution.

# Azure Load Balancer

A load balancer resource can be either a public load balancer (also called an external load balancer) or a private load balancer (also called an internal load balancer) within the context of the virtual network. Azure Load Balancer has an inbound and an out-bound feature set. The Load Balancer resource functionality is expressed in several concepts: a frontend, a rule, a health probe, and a backend pool definition. Azure Load Balancer maps new flows to healthy backend instances.

Azure Load Balancer operates on Layer 4 and is available in two versions. The Stan-dard load balancer enables you to scale your applications and create high availability for small-scale deployments to large and complex multizone architectures, allowing for up to 1,000 backend virtual machines. The Basic load balancer does not support HTTPS health probes, is limited to a maximum of 300 backend virtual machines, and is not suitable for production workloads. The Basic-tier load balancer is free to use, whereas the Standard tier has a pricing model associated with it. You might use a Basic-tier load balancer for basic load balancing needs in development environments, where the backend pool is small and you're not concerned about active HTTPS health checks. The Standard tier includes an SLA, multidimensional metrics, and more advanced configuration to frontends and rules.

As Azure Load Balancer is a Layer 4 device, the connection between a client and a backend server is a direct connection. In the configuration of a public Load Balancer in front of private VMs, the backend VM sees a connection coming from a public IP address to its private IP and the Load Balancer is acting as an inbound Network Address Translation (NAT) device that has load-balancing capabilities. The frontend IP address, together with the port number of incoming traffic, is mapped by the Load Balancer to a backend pool. The backend pool may consist of a number of direct VM IP addresses or a scale set, along with a corresponding destination port. By applying load-balancing rules, you can distribute specific types of traffic across multiple VMs or services. For example, you can use an Azure Load Balancer to handle traffic for multiple types of connections for different application types to distribute load among horizontally scaled machines with a single load balancer.

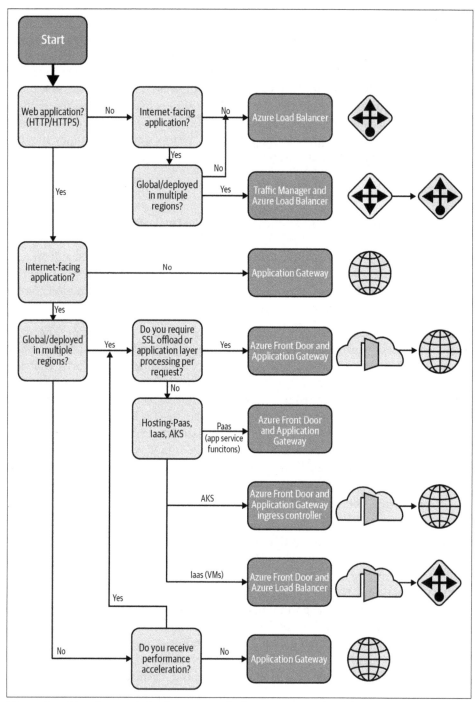

*Figure 2-1. Flowchart to help determine which Azure native load-balancing service or combination of services may be best for your use case.*

In the scenario in which a backend service needs to connect outbound, its connections are routed through the Load Balancer's public frontend IP address. This functionality is called Source Network Address Translation, or SNAT. In a way, it's a reverse load balancer: connections from multiple machines are coming from the same public IP. This is called masquerading, where the machine in the middle hides the real client IP from the destination of the connection. Masquerading is not done on inbound connections, which is why the backend VM sees the connection directly from the client. If a backend VM needs to provide a return port to the client to reconnect, Azure Load Balancers can be configured to enable port access translation (PAT) and allocate ephemeral ports to each backend VM in a pool that will direct the client directly to a specific backend VM.

A few example scenarios of Azure Load Balancer usage:

*Non-HTTP(S) load balancing*
Load balancing of any protocols built on top of TCP/UDP, including but not limited to HTTP(S).

*Public-facing load balancer*
Horizontally scaled or HA private application servers hosted in a virtual network need to have incoming loads from the internet distributed between them.

*Private load balancer*
Provides a single private endpoint to load balance over an HA service or one that is scaled horizontally.

*Outbound connections*
When an HA or horizontally scaled application needs to initiate connections outbound while maintaining a single ingress and egress point.

Figure 2-2 depicts the public-facing Load Balancer scenario, in which an Azure Load Balancer is distributing load for an Azure VM Scale Set that consists of multiple VMs.

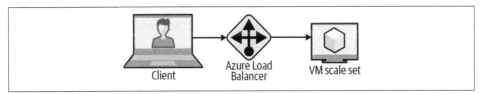

*Figure 2-2. Visual of code build of solution using Azure Load Balancer.*

# Azure Application Gateway for Load Balancing

Azure Application Gateway is a Layer 7 request router. Azure Application Gateway is a proxy: it receives the request from the client and makes a request to the backend service on the client's behalf. Unlike the Azure Load Balancer, there are two connections in this scenario. One connection is between the client and Azure Application Gateway, and the other is between Azure Application Gateway and the backend. By receiving the request from the client, decrypting it in the case of HTTPS, and understanding the HTTP protocol, the Azure Application Gateway can inspect the request and then block, redirect, and route accordingly.

Routing rules are applied that can direct the request to different backend pools based on HTTP information such as URI. This is perfect for the microservice architecture, as it enables you to have one endpoint listening for requests, matching a route prefix, and directing the request to the correct microservice. The backend pool can consist of IP addresses, fully qualified domain names (FQDNs), VMs, Scale Sets, and additional App Services. When multiple entities exist within a single pool, they're load balanced with a round-robin algorithm. Only entities considered healthy will be sent requests.

The health of a backend is checked through the use of a health probe. A health probe is a configuration that tells Azure Application Gateway to periodically make a specific request to all entities in a backend pool wand to expect a specific response code and optionally a response body match in return. If an entity in a backend pool fails its health probe, Azure Application Gateway will no longer send it client requests but will continue to monitor it with a health probe.

Session affinity can be configured for Azure Application Gateway. Session affinity will cause Azure Application Gateway to generate a cookie for the client that will instruct Azure Application Gateway to direct subsequent requests from this client to a specific entity within a backend pool. This affinity happens at the pool layer, so that if a request from the same client routes to a different backend pool, the client would receive another cookie, binding them to a separate backend entity in the pool the request is served from.

Rules are mapped to listeners, which receive incoming requests. Listeners can be mapped by IP or hostname. Each listener can be attached to many rules, and those rules map to backend pools. By using separate listeners, you can route the same URI path for two different hostnames to two separate backend pools with one Azure Application Gateway. It also means that you can use the same backend pool for different offerings listening on separate hostnames.

Azure Application Gateway can also rewrite request URI and headers before performing the request to the backend services. This feature might be useful when the frontend API routing relies on prefixes but the backend service doesn't use the prefix in its route, or when an application's routes do not fit the overall scheme of the rest of your API.

Azure Application Gateway provides the very valuable feature of Layer 7 request routing through a scalable managed regional service. With a vast amount of configuration possibilities, Azure Application Gateway is meant to be the traffic cop that stops and directs traffic between a client and your application.

# Azure Web Application Firewall (WAF) with ModSecurity

One feature of Azure Application Gateway is the ability to apply Web Application Firewall (WAF) policies, which provide your applications with protection from common vulnerabilities and exploits like SQL injection or cross-site scripting (XSS) attacks. A WAF policy requires at least one Azure managed rule set and optionally can be configured with custom rules. Within a managed rule set, particular rules can be turned on or off. WAF policies can be set to enforce and actively block violating requests or to passively monitor and record security events. Individual custom rules can be set to block or monitor as well.

Azure WAF policies utilize the open source, cross-platform WAF ModSecurity, which uses the Core Rule Set of the Open Web Application Security Project (OWASP) (*https://oreil.ly/JoVPm*). The OWASP rule set is community supported and regularly updated. You will see in the WAF policies that there are multiple versions of the OWASP rule set.

Azure WAF policies do not expose the full functionality of ModSecurity but do allow you to filter requests through rules to match variables from a request to policies to block, flag, or deny requests. A Layer 7 router is the perfect point in the stack to block malicious requests before they ever reach the application server. This protects your resources and reduces stress on your business logic layer. Figure 2-3 depicts how Azure routes a request through a WAF policy.

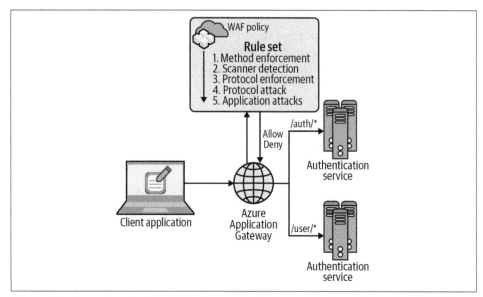

*Figure 2-3. Azure Application Gateway processing a request through an Azure WAF policy.*

## Azure Front Door

Azure Front Door provides the ability to configure, manage, and monitor global routing for all your web traffic by optimizing performance and failover for high availability at a global scale. Using something called *split TCP anycast protocol*, the service ensures that your users always connect to the nearest Front Door point of presence (POP). Split TCP works by breaking a connection with a high round trip into smaller segments. Front Door environments are placed closer to end users, and the connections are terminated inside the Front Door, which means a TCP connection with an expensive round trip to a backend is split into two TCP connections. Anycast is a network addressing and routing methodology where a destination has multiple routing paths to two or more endpoint destinations—the ideal approach is determined based on the number of hops, distance, or network latency. Front Door leverages anycast for DNS and HTTP traffic to ensure user traffic goes to the environment with the fewest hops—the DNS layer being how a client selects a Front Door endpoint, and the HTTP layer being how Front Door selects a backend to serve the request.

To do this, Front Door organizes environments into rings. The outer ring has environments that are closer to users, which means they offer lower latency, while the inner ring can handle the failover of the outer ring environment if an issue were to occur. This configuration ensures that end-user requests always reach the closest Front Door environment but that traffic gets moved to a healthy environment if the outer ring environment fails. Figure 2-4 depicts Azure Front Door points of presence organized into inner and outer rings.

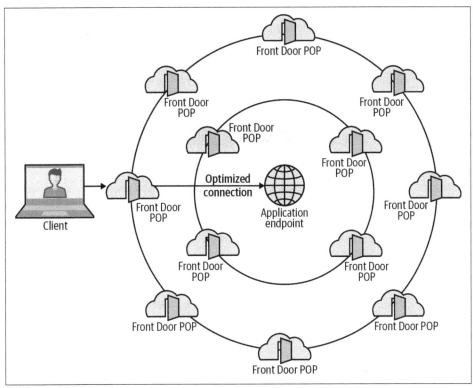

*Figure 2-4. Azure Front Door points of presence organized into rings: the client connects to the closest healthy point of presence, which makes an optimized connection to the application endpoint.*

Front Door automatically triggers health probes to check on your backend services for latency and availability—if a health probe detects that a backend is down, it will quickly provide automatic failover. The load balancing performed by Front Door is like a least latency algorithm. Front Door is useful when clients are spread out globally because of its split TCP functionality; its load balancing is useful when you're running the same service in multiple regions. The failover capabilities allow for planned maintenance without downtime by switching load to another installation of the service. We'll discuss further applications of Front Door and integration with NGINX in Chapter 5.

# Azure Traffic Manager for Cloud-Based DNS Load Balancing

Azure Traffic Manager is a DNS-based load manager that directs the request to the proper endpoints based on method and endpoint health. Traffic Manager offers multiple routing methods and endpoint monitoring tools suitable for a wide range of application or failover needs. Table 2-2 shows what each method offers.

*Table 2-2. Azure Traffic Manager routing methods*

| Method | Description |
|---|---|
| Priority | Uses a primary service endpoint for all traffic with a set of backups for failover |
| Weighted | Distributes traffic across all endpoints based on configured weights |
| Performance | For endpoints in different geographic locations, routes traffic to the endpoint closest to a user based on latency |
| Geographic | Routes based on the geographic origin of the DNS query |
| Multivalue | When selected, returns all healthy endpoints; used for profiles limited to IPv4/IPv6 addresses as endpoints |
| Subnet | User IP address ranges mapped to a specific endpoint within a profile; endpoint returned is the one mapped to source IP of the request |

Endpoint health and automatic endpoint failover monitoring are included in all Traffic Manager profiles. Only one routing method can be used by a single profile, but the method can be changed at any time without downtime. You can combine routing profiles with nested Traffic Manager profiles.

## Priority Traffic Routing

For a high-reliability service deployment, you should configure one or more services as failover endpoints. That way, if your primary service goes down, traffic is routed to the failover endpoints based on the priority set to each of the secondary (failover) services.

In Figure 2-5, when "Primary Priority 1" fails, all traffic is automatically redirected to "Failover A Priority 2." The client's browser makes a DNS request that is routed to Traffic Manager, which evaluates priority and status. The highest priority endpoint being degraded causes Traffic Manager to respond with the DNS response for Failover A, as it is online and of the next priority precedence. The client then makes a request directly to the Failover A endpoint. Failover B is online but has less precedence than Failover A.

The priority can be any value between 1 and 1,000 with lower values representing higher priorities. Remember that if you do not define a priority, a default priority will be automatically assigned based on endpoint order.

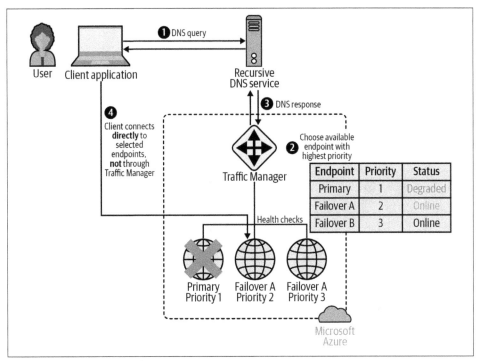

*Figure 2-5. Priority Traffic Routing.*

## Weighted Traffic Routing

With this method, a weight is preassigned to each endpoint, and every incoming request is routed based on these values. For example, if Endpoint 1 Weight = 30%, Endpoint 2 Weight = 20%, and Endpoint 3 Weight = 50%, 30% of the traffic will be routed to Endpoint 1, 20% will be routed to Endpoint 2, and, finally, half of all traffic will be routed to Endpoint 3. If you assign an equal weight distribution, every endpoint will receive the same amount of traffic.

Pilot scenarios for when you want to test a new deployment of your application (including some new features or an upgrade, let's say) frequently use this method. You start by deploying the new feature or upgrade to one of your endpoints, assign it a lower weight such as 10% or 20%, and monitor how it behaves from a systems and user behavior standpoint. If everything is running smoothly, you can increase the weight, and then, once it's confirmed that the release is successful, deploy to all other nodes. Intrinsically, deploying in this phased manner avoids Big Bang approaches and diminishes the severity of any issues.

Figure 2-6 shows how weighted traffic routing can be used in a multiregion Azure deployment when one of the regions is degraded. Region A and Region B have equal weights, while Test A has a much lower weight. When the client's DNS request is made, the request is directed to Traffic Manager, which will respond to the request with respect to the defined weight ratio. As Region A is considered unhealthy, it's likely that the result of the DNS query will be Region B with respect to a 50/5 ratio. The client's connection will then be directed to the Region B endpoint.

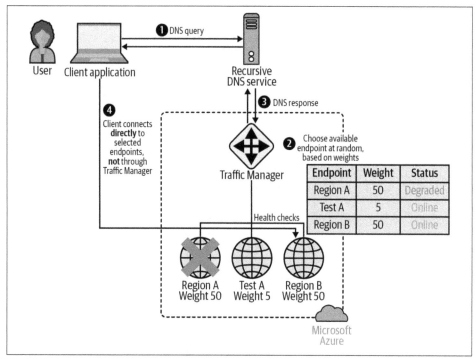

*Figure 2-6. Weighted traffic routing in a multiregion Azure deployment.*

## Performance Traffic Routing

The performance routing method is used when application responsiveness is a top priority. With this method, you deploy endpoints in two or more locations, and traffic is routed to the closest location. "Closest" is not necessarily defined in terms of distance but by measuring network latency. To determine which endpoint has the lowest network latency, the Traffic Manager service maintains an Internet Latency Table to track round-trip time between IP address ranges and each data center.

Figure 2-7 uses a diagram to visualize performance routing for a multiregion Azure deployment, when the primary region is degraded. Traffic Manager keeps a lookup table based on public IP ranges and the average round-trip latency of DNS requests from those ranges. When the DNS request is made from the client and routed to Traffic Manager, Traffic Manager looks up the client's IP address and finds that Endpoint 1 has the lowest average latency for clients in this IP range. Endpoint 1 is considered degraded, and therefore Traffic Manager responds to the DNS request with values for Endpoint 2, because it is the least latent endpoint in service.

Remember, you can use a Nested Traffic Manager profile to define a different traffic distribution within a region or to define a failover sequence for when all endpoints in the closest region are degraded.

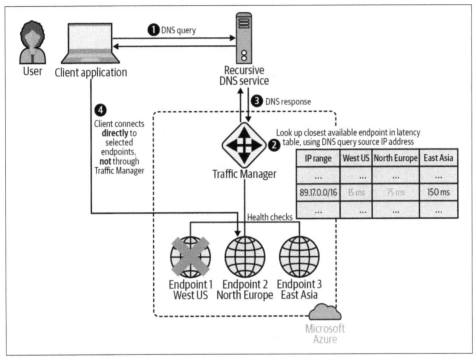

*Figure 2-7. Performance routing in a multiregion Azure deployment.*

## Geographic Traffic Routing

Geographic traffic routing applies rules that map client IP addresses to geographical regions. The routing is done by applying rules to match specific regions and sending requests to the appropriate endpoint. This is helpful for keeping requests and data within geographies, to comply with GDPR, for example.

The following are the types of rule matches that can be used:

- Any region
- Specific region: Africa, Middle East, Australia/Pacific
- Country/Region: Ireland, Peru
- State/Province: United States–Florida, Australia–Sydney, Canada–Toronto (this granularity level is only supported for the US, Canada, and Australia)

Figure 2-8 shows how Traffic Manager would route the client to a specific endpoint based on user geography. When the client's browser queries for DNS, Traffic Manager will determine the user's location based on the client's IP address and match the endpoint value returned based on rules applied. In this scenario, Traffic Manager responds with Endpoint 1; however, if Endpoint 1 is degraded, Endpoint 2 would act as a catchall. When Traffic Manager responds, the client connects directly to the endpoint.

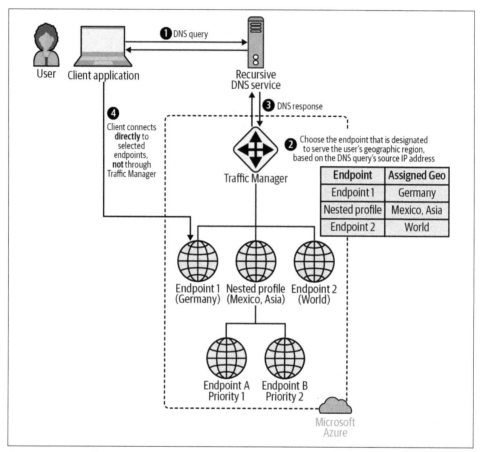

*Figure 2-8. Traffic Manager is configured to map users geographic locations to specific endpoints.*

With geographic routing, if an endpoint is assigned a region or set of regions, that endpoint will receive all requests coming from the region(s). Keep in mind that a region can be mapped only to a single endpoint, and thus the Traffic Manager service will return the endpoint regardless of endpoint health. You should always use this method with Nested type endpoints that have child profiles of at least two endpoints each; otherwise you can suffer downtime.

# Designing Highly Available Systems

When designing large-scale applications that are highly available, remember that you will need to use several of these load-balancing components together. As an example, Figure 2-9 shows a geographically distributed and load-balanced application.

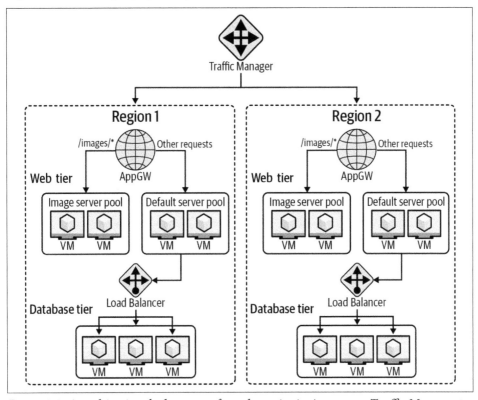

*Figure 2-9. A multiregion deployment of a web service in Azure uses Traffic Manager to direct clients to a particular region based on the routing rules applied.*

Here, Traffic Manager will route any incoming request to the appropriate region based on performance. Once the request is received at the nearest data center, Azure Application Gateway chooses which application server to fetch the response from. The Application Gateway decrypts the HTTP request and uses the URI of the request to route the request to a backend server pool. The request to the backend service may be re-encrypted for transit. The backend service then makes a connection to a database tier through an Azure Load Balancer.

## Conclusion

In this chapter, we discussed the managed load-balancing options in Azure. There are many available options that provide slightly different solutions at different layers. These services complement one another, and are often layered to provide a more comprehensive solution to fit your and your client's needs.

Chapter 3 will dive into NGINX and NGINX Plus and how to deploy them in Azure in detail.

# NGINX and NGINX Plus on Azure

NGINX, Inc., a company that is now part of F5 Networks, shares its name with its leading product, NGINX. NGINX has two versions: an Open Source software solution, OSS, and a commercial solution, Plus. These two versions dominate the world of application delivery controllers, both on-premises and in the cloud. In Azure, many companies are trying to decide between the Azure native managed services discussed in the previous chapter and solutions they already use and trust from their on-premises environments. This chapter will explore the similarities and differences between NGINX OSS and NGINX Plus and how to deploy them using the Azure Portal, PowerShell, and Terraform. In the next chapter, we'll cover comparisons between NGINX solutions and Azure managed solutions.

Both NGINX and NGINX Plus can fit into your web application landscape as a load balancer for TCP and UDP, but they also can fill the need for a more advanced HTTP(S) application delivery controller. NGINX and NGINX Plus operate at Layer 7 for all types of load balancing. You might employ NGINX or NGINX Plus as an entry point and HTTP(S) request router for your application, or as a load balancer for a service that uses a protocol that is not HTTP, such as database read replicas.

## NGINX Versus NGINX Plus

NGINX Open Source software, or NGINX OSS, is free open source software, whereas NGINX Plus is a commercial product that offers advanced features and enterprise-level support as licensed software by NGINX, Inc.

NGINX combines the functionality of a high-performance web server, a powerful load balancer, and a highly scalable caching layer to create the ideal end-to-end platform for your web applications. NGINX Plus is built on top of NGINX OSS. For the sake of clarity, if the product NGINX is ever referenced in this book without the explicit denotation of "Plus," the feature set being described is available in both versions, as all of the OSS version capabilities are available in NGINX Plus.

For organizations currently using NGINX OSS, NGINX Plus provides your data plane with "off the shelf" advanced features such as intelligent session persistence, JSON Web Token (JWT) and OpenID Connect integration, advanced monitoring statistics, and clustering abilities. These features enable your data plane to integrate more deeply with your application layer, provide deeper insight into your application traffic flow, and enable state-aware high availability. NGINX Plus also enables access to a knowledgable support team that specializes in data plane technology and NGINX Plus implementation. We've personally met some of these support engineers at the NGINX conference, NGINX.conf, and our conversations were deep and introspective about the current state of application delivery on the modern web.

For organizations currently using hardware-based load balancers, NGINX Plus provides a full set of ADC features in a much more flexible way, through means of a software form factor, with a cost-effective subscription. We've worked with a number of data plane solutions that were hardware-based but pivoted their business to virtual appliance when the cloud really took hold. A common theme for virtual network appliances is that their operating systems are based in BSD rather than Linux. Years ago, BSD's networking stack had an advantage over Linux; this margin has since shrunk, and when running on vitalized infrastructure, the margin between them is even more diminished. Maintaining another set of tools to manage a separate kernel type is, in our opinion, not worth the effort. In a move to the cloud, you want to manage all VMs through the same methodology. If a specific set of VMs does not fit the mold of your management model, it requires an exception; that if condition may exist in your configuration code or your compliance documentation, neither of which is necessary given that capable software-based data plane controllers provide the same or greater functionality.

Table 3-1 shows the NGINX Plus feature sets compared to those of NGINX OSS. You can get more information on the differences between NGINX products at *https://nginx.com*.

*Table 3-1. Comparison of highlighted NGINX OSS and NGINX Plus features*

| Feature type | Feature | NGINX OSS | NGINX Plus |
|---|---|---|---|
| **Load balancer** | HTTP/TCP/UDP support | X | X |
| | Layer 7 request routing | X | X |
| | Active health checks | | X |
| | Sophisticated session persistence | | X |
| | DNS SRV support (service discovery) | | X |
| **Content cache** | Static/dynamic content caching | X | X |
| | Cache-purging API | | X |

| Feature type | Feature | NGINX OSS | NGINX Plus |
|---|---|:---:|:---:|
| **Web server/reverse proxy** | Origin server for static content | X | X |
| | Reverse proxy protocols: TCP, UDP, HTTP, FastCGI, uwsgi, gRPC | X | X |
| | HTTP/2 gateway | X | X |
| | HTTP/2 server push | X | X |
| **Security controls** | HTTP Basic Authentication | X | X |
| | HTTP authentication subrequests | X | X |
| | IP address-based subrequests | X | X |
| | Rate limiting | X | X |
| | Dual-stack RSA/ECC SSL/TLS offload | X | X |
| | ModSecurity 3.0 support | X | X |
| | TLS 1.3 support | X | X |
| | JWT authentication | | X |
| | OpenID Connect SSO | | X |
| | NGINX App Protect (WAF) | | X |
| **Monitoring** | Syslog | X | X |
| | AppDynamics, Datadog, Dynatrace plug-ins | X | X |
| | Basic Status Metrics | X | X |
| | Advanced Metrics with Dashboard 90+ metrics | | X |
| **High availability** | Behind Azure Load Balancer | X | X |
| | Configuration synchronization | | X |
| | State sharing: sticky-learn session persistence, rate limiting, key-value stores | | X |
| **Programmability** | NGINX JavaScript module | X | X |
| | Third-party Lea and Perl modules | X | X |
| | Custom C module | X | X |
| | Seamless reconfiguration through process reload | X | X |
| | NGINX Plus API dynamic configuration | | X |
| | Key-value store | | X |
| | Dynamic reconfiguration without process reloads | | X |

# Installing NGINX OSS and NGINX Plus

Both NGINX OSS and NGINX Plus are widely available to download and install from a variety of sources. This flexibility allows you to find and use the deployment option that best suits your needs. For instance, you can install via prebuilt Azure virtual machine images available in the Azure Marketplace, manually on a virtual machine, or through the Azure Resource Center with PowerShell. We'll walk through the installation process for these settings next.

## Installing via Azure Marketplace

Azure Marketplace is a software repository for prebuilt and configured Azure resources from independent software vendors (ISVs). You will find open source and enterprise applications that have been certified and optimized to run on Azure.

NGINX, Inc., provides the latest release of NGINX Plus in Azure Marketplace as a virtual machine (VM) image. NGINX OSS is not available from NGINX, Inc., as an Azure Marketplace VM image, but there are several options available from other ISVs in Azure Marketplace.

Searching for "NGINX" in Azure Marketplace will produce several results, as shown in Figure 3-1.

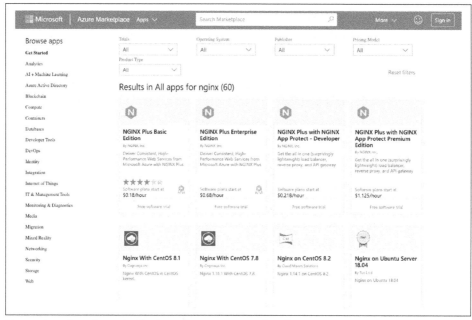

*Figure 3-1. Searching for "NGINX" in Azure Marketplace.*

You will see several results besides the official NGINX Plus VM images from NGINX, Inc., such as the following examples from other ISVs for NGINX OSS:

- NGINX Web Server (CentOS 7)
- NGINX Web Server on Windows Server 2016
- NGINX Ingress Controller Container Image

There are currently four options available from NGINX, Inc. You can choose from different tiers of NGINX Plus with or without NGINX App Protect, as shown in Figure 3-2. The tiers correspond to the support level and readiness for production usage.

*Figure 3-2. NGINX Plus in the Azure Marketplace.*

The initial page presented is the Overview page, which summarizes the NGINX Plus software functionality and pricing. For more details, click the "Plans" link. There are a number of plans. The plans simply provide a way to select the base OS you'd like NGINX Plus to run on. Select a plan and press the Create button to be taken to the Azure virtual machine creation process. To avoid confusion, the plan is not associated with cost for the NGINX Plus image, only the base OS; the cost associated with the NGINX Plus Marketplace image is the same independent of the base OS.

The Azure VM creation process using the Azure Portal follows seven standard steps, with explanations for each step on the Azure Portal page in the following areas: Basics, Disks, Networking, Management, Advanced (Settings), and Tags. The final step allows you to review and approve any associated costs before the VM is built. These seven steps are displayed in Figure 3-3.

When selecting a size for your VM, a cost will be associated. This includes the cost for the NGINX Plus software.

It is recommended that an Azure availability set of two or more VMs be used to provide high availability in the case of planned system maintenance by Azure or as a safeguard against one VM becoming unavailable. Zone redundancy, if available in the region, is also suggested, as it protects against Azure zone failure and maintenance outages.

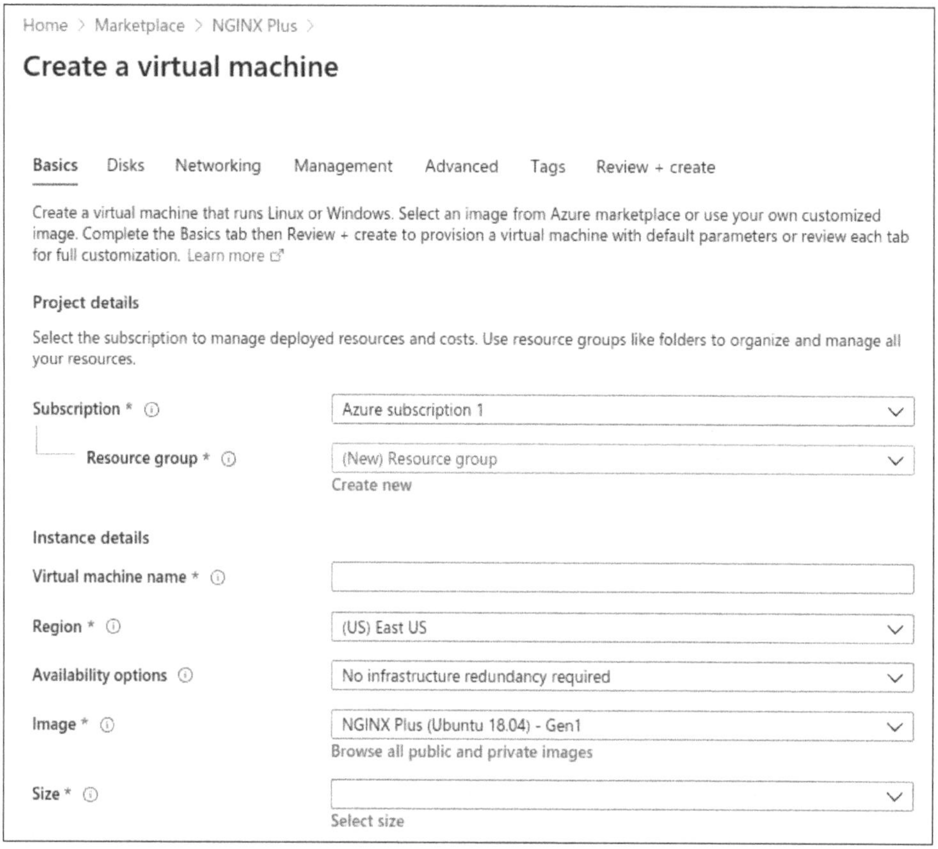

*Figure 3-3. Creating a virtual machine using the Azure Portal.*

You will need to manually create endpoints to support HTTPS (port 443) and HTTP (port 80) traffic in the Azure Portal to enable access to the NGINX Plus VM. For more information, see "How to set up endpoints on a Linux classic virtual machine in Azure" (*https://oreil.ly/qbdpq*) in the Azure documentation.

NGINX Plus will start automatically and load its default start page once the VM starts. You can use a web browser to navigate to the VM's IP address or DNS name. You can also check the running status of NGINX Plus by logging in to the VM and running the following command:

```
$ /etc/init.d/nginx status
```

Azure virtual machine scale sets (VMSSs) let you create and manage a group of identical load-balanced VMs. VMSSs provide redundancy and improved performance by automatically scaling up or down based on workloads or a predefined schedule.

To scale NGINX Plus, create a public or internal Azure Load Balancer with a VMSS. You can deploy the NGINX Plus VM to the VMSS and then configure the Azure Load Balancer for the desired rules, ports, and protocols for allowed traffic to the backend pool.

The cost of running NGINX Plus is a combination of the selected software plan charges plus the Azure infrastructure costs for the VMs on which you will be running the software. There are no additional costs for VMSSs, but you do pay for the underlying compute resources. The actual Azure infrastructure price might vary if you have enterprise agreements or other discounts.

Using NGINX Plus from the Azure Marketplace enables you to scale your NGINX Plus layer on demand without having to procure more licenses, as the software cost is built into the Marketplace with a pay-per-usage model. You may want to procure a couple of machine licenses for your base footprint to enter the support contract with NGINX, Inc., and then use the Marketplace for burst capacity.

## Installing Manually on VMs

In some instances, you may want to install NGINX manually on an Azure VM. Example use cases include a need for modules not included in a Marketplace image, for extra packages, for advanced configurations, for the latest version of NGINX, or for bootstrapping to be tightly controlled by configuration management.

The process for installing NGINX OSS or NGINX Plus on an Azure VM is no different than for installing them on any other hosting platform because NGINX is software that runs on top of any Linux distribution.

In Azure, your configuration should be repeatable through automation so that you can scale as necessary. You can either manually build a VM and take an image of it, so that you can use the image in an Azure Scale Set, or automate the installation through scripting or configuration management. You can also combine the two methods, so that automation builds VM images.

VM images will be ready to serve the client faster because the software is already installed. Installing at boot time provides flexibility, as the configuration can change without having to create images, but it takes longer to become ready because it has to install the software. A hybrid approach should be considered in which an image is made with the software installed, but configuration management brings the configuration up to date at boot time.

When installing NGINX OSS, we always make sure to use the NGINX official package repository for the Linux distribution that we're using. This ensures that we always have the latest version with the most up-to-date features and security fixes. You can learn how to install from the official repository by visiting the "Supported Distributions and Versions" page of the NGINX documentation (*https://oreil.ly/u4RX8*).

## Installing NGINX OSS via Azure Resource Manager and PowerShell

Azure Resource Manager (ARM) templates are a native Azure automation process that uses declarative state JSON objects to build resources within Azure. This process is the default option for Azure Infrastructure as Code (IaC) and allows you to check your templates into source control.

There are currently no prebuilt ARM templates or PowerShell scripts available from NGINX, Inc. However, there is nothing preventing the creation of a Resource Manager template and PowerShell script based on your custom deployment requirements for Azure and using your previously created custom VM images.

The following provides an example of creating an Ubuntu 16.04 LTS marketplace image from Canonical along with the NGINX OSS web server using Azure Cloud Shell and the Azure PowerShell module.

Open Azure Cloud Shell, and perform the following steps in Azure PowerShell.

First, let's use `ssh-keygen` to create a Secure Shell (SSH) key pair. Accept all the defaults by pressing the Enter key:

```
ssh-keygen -t rsa -b 2048
# RSA private key will be saved as id_rsa
# RSA public key will be saved as id_rsa.pub
# Created in directory: '/home/azureuser/.ssh'
```

Before we can run any Azure CLI commands, we'll need to be logged in. Use the following command to receive a link and an access code that you paste into a browser to verify your Azure identity:

```
Connect-AzAccount
```

Next, create an Azure resource group by using `New-AzResourceGroup`:

```
New-AzResourceGroup `
-Name "nginx-rg" `
-Location "EastUS2"
```

Using the `New-AzVirtualNetworkSubnetConfig` command, you can now create a subnet config object, which will be used when creating a new Azure Virtual Network using the `New-AzVirtualNetwork` command. After those are created, `New-AzPublicIpAddress` will create an IP address to use with the NGINX VM:

```
# Create a subnet configuration
$subnetConfig = New-AzVirtualNetworkSubnetConfig `
-Name "nginx-Subnet" `
-AddressPrefix 192.168.1.0/24

# Create a virtual network
$vnet = New-AzVirtualNetwork `
-ResourceGroupName "nginx-rg" `
-Location "EastUS2" `
-Name "nginxVNET" `
-AddressPrefix 192.168.0.0/16 `
-Subnet $subnetConfig

# Create a public IP address
# and specify a DNS name
$pip = New-AzPublicIpAddress `
-ResourceGroupName "nginx-rg" `
-Location "EastUS2" `
-AllocationMethod Static `
-IdleTimeoutInMinutes 4 `
-Name "nginxpublicdns$(Get-Random)"
```

Though doing so is optional, it is best practice to add an Azure network security group (NSG) (New-AzNetworkSecurityGroup) along with traffic rules using New-AzNetworkSecurityRuleConfig:

```
# Create an inbound NSG rule for port 22
$nsgRuleSSH = New-AzNetworkSecurityRuleConfig `
-Name "nginxNSGRuleSSH" `
-Protocol "Tcp" `
-Direction "Inbound" `
-Priority 1000 `
-SourceAddressPrefix * `
-SourcePortRange * `
-DestinationAddressPrefix * `
-DestinationPortRange 22 `
-Access "Allow"

# Create an inbound NSG rule for port 80
$nsgRuleWeb = New-AzNetworkSecurityRuleConfig `
-Name "nginxNSGRuleWWW" `
-Protocol "Tcp" `
-Direction "Inbound" `
-Priority 1001 `
-SourceAddressPrefix * `
-SourcePortRange * `
-DestinationAddressPrefix * `
-DestinationPortRange 80 `
-Access "Allow"

# Create a network security group (NSG)
$nsg = New-AzNetworkSecurityGroup `
```

```
-ResourceGroupName "nginx-rg" `
-Location "EastUS2" `
-Name "nginxNSG" `
-SecurityRules $nsgRuleSSH,$nsgRuleWeb

# Create a virtual network card and
# associate it with the public IP
# address and NSG
$nic = New-AzNetworkInterface `
-Name "nginxNIC" `
-ResourceGroupName "nginx-rg" `
-Location "EastUS2" `
-SubnetId $vnet.Subnets[0].Id `
-PublicIpAddressId $pip.Id `
-NetworkSecurityGroupId $nsg.Id
```

PowerShell allows you to quickly build a VM while specifying VM attributes such as memory, vCPUs, disks, and network cards based on the VM image options available on Azure. The following is the configuration of the VM suitable for our example:

```
# Define a credential object make sure that your password is unique and secure
$securePassword = ConvertTo-SecureString `
'MySuperSecurePasswordWith#sAndSymbols*)23' -AsPlainText -Force
$cred = New-Object `
System.Management.Automation.PSCredential("azureuser",
$securePassword)

# Create a virtual machine configuration
$vmConfig = New-AzVMConfig `
-VMName "nginxVM" `
-VMSize "Standard_B1s" | `
Set-AzVMOperatingSystem `
-Linux `
-ComputerName "nginxVM" `
-Credential $cred `
-DisablePasswordAuthentication | `
Set-AzVMSourceImage `
-PublisherName "Canonical" `
-Offer "UbuntuServer" `
-Skus "16.04-LTS" `
-Version "latest" | `
Add-AzVMNetworkInterface `
-Id $nic.Id

# Configure the SSH key
$sshPublicKey = cat ~/.ssh/id_rsa.pub
Add-AzVMSshPublicKey `
-VM $vmconfig `
-KeyData $sshPublicKey `
-Path "/home/azureuser/.ssh/authorized_keys"
```

Next, combine the previous configuration definitions to create a new VM by using New-AzVM:

```
New-AzVM `
-ResourceGroupName "nginx-rg" `
-Location eastus2 -VM $vmConfig
```

Using SSH, connect to the VM after it is created by using the public IP displayed by the following code:

```
Get-AzPublicIpAddress `
-ResourceGroupName "nginx-rg" | `
Select "IpAddress"
```

In the Azure Cloud Shell or your local bash shell, paste the SSH connection command into the shell to create an SSH session, using the login username **azureuser** when prompted. If an optional passphrase is used, please enter it when prompted:

```
ssh azureuser@<vm-public-ip>
```

From your SSH session, update your package sources and then install the latest NGINX OSS package by running the following as root or with sudo:

```
echo \
 "deb http://nginx.org/packages/mainline/ubuntu/ xenial nginx" \
 > /etc/apt/sources.list.d/nginx.list

echo \
 "deb-src http://nginx.org/packages/mainline/ubuntu/ xenial nginx" \
 >> /etc/apt/sources.list.d/nginx.list

wget http://nginx.org/keys/nginx_signing.key
apt-key add nginx_signing.key
apt-get update
apt-get -y install nginx

# Test NGINX is installed
nginx -v

# Start NGINX - it's enabled to start at boot by default
/etc/init.d/nginx start
```

You will need to use a web browser to test the loading of the default NGINX OSS start page, which is the public IP address of the VM you've created. To exit the SSH session, type exit when done.

Once you have completed this process, you can us the Remove-AzResourceGroup cmdlet to remove the resource group, VM, virtual network, and all other Azure resources to avoid incurring ongoing charges:

```
Remove-AzResourceGroup `
-Name "nginx-rg"
```

# Deploying Infrastructure for NGINX OSS via Terraform

In this section, we will deploy a Linux virtual machine with NGINX OSS using Terraform. We will show two examples: one for Debian and Ubuntu, and another for CentOS and Red Hat. Items common to both of them are the provider and the network that will provide the starting point for installing NGINX OSS.

### If You're Unfamiliar with Terraform

You can learn about Terraform by reading the Introduction to Terraform (*https://oreil.ly/02Cvx*) document, or by going through the "Get Started – Azure" guide (*https://oreil.ly/dN_jb*). If you are using Azure Cloud Shell, the "Configure Terraform using Azure Cloud Shell" document (*https://oreil.ly/O5RJs*) may be useful.

### The provider

The first step is to create the provider file. The provider is used to interact with the Azure APIs.

We create a file called *provider-main.tf*, which is used to create the interaction with Terraform and the Azure providers:

```
# Define Terraform provider
terraform {
  required_version = ">= 0.12"
}

# Configure the Azure provider
provider "azurerm" {
  environment = "public"
  version     = ">= 2.15.0"
  features {}
  # It is important that the following values of these variables
  #  NEVER be written to source control, and therefore should not be
  #  hard-coded with defaults and should always come from the local
  #  environment
  subscription_id = var.azure-subscription-id
  client_id       = var.azure-client-id
  client_secret   = var.azure-client-secret
  tenant_id       = var.azure-tenant-id
}
```

Next, we create a file called *provider-variables.tf*, which is used to manage the authentication variables of the Azure provider:

```
variable "azure-subscription-id" {
  type        = string
  description = "Azure Subscription ID"
}
```

```
variable "azure-client-id" {
  type        = string
  description = "Azure Client ID"
}

variable "azure-client-secret" {
  type        = string
  description = "Azure Client Secret"
}

variable "azure-tenant-id" {
  type        = string
  description = "Azure Tenant ID"
}
```

## The network

The next step is to create the resource group that will host all of our Azure resources. A VNET, and a subnet within the VNET, will also be created. The subnet will host our virtual machine.

We create a file called *network-main.tf* to describe these resources:

```
# Create a resource group
resource "azurerm_resource_group" "network-rg" {
  name     = "nginx-network-rg"
  location = var.location
}

# Create the network VNET
resource "azurerm_virtual_network" "network-vnet" {
  name                = "nginx-network-vnet"
  address_space       = [var.network-vnet-cidr]
  resource_group_name = azurerm_resource_group.network-rg.name
  location            = azurerm_resource_group.network-rg.location
}

# Create a subnet for VM
resource "azurerm_subnet" "vm-subnet" {
  name                 = "nginx-vm-subnet"
  address_prefixes     = [var.vm-subnet-cidr]
  virtual_network_name = azurerm_virtual_network.network-vnet.name
  resource_group_name  = azurerm_resource_group.network-rg.name
}
```

Then we create a file called *network-variables.tf* to manage network variables:

```
variable "location" {
  type        = string
  description = "Azure Region"
  default     = "eastus"
}
```

```
variable "network-vnet-cidr" {
  type        = string
  description = "The CIDR of the network VNET"
}

variable "vm-subnet-cidr" {
  type        = string
  description = "The CIDR for the vm subnet"
}
```

## Security

In this section, we will create an Azure NSG (network security group) to protect our virtual machine. The security group will allow inbound traffic in ports 22 (SSH), 80 (HTTP), and 443 (HTTPS).

**Opening SSH to the Internet**

For brevity, the following code will allow SSH connections from anywhere on the internet. You should determine your own needs for SSH access and restrict access accordingly.

Create a file called *security-main.tf* and add the following code:

```
# Create Network Security Group
resource "azurerm_network_security_group" "nginx-vm-nsg" {
  depends_on=[azurerm_resource_group.network-rg]

  name                = "nginxvm-nsg"
  location            = azurerm_resource_group.network-rg.location
  resource_group_name = azurerm_resource_group.network-rg.name

  # Allows inbound SSH from entire internet!
  security_rule {
    name                       = "Allow-SSH"
    description                = "Allow SSH"
    priority                   = 100
    direction                  = "Inbound"
    access                     = "Allow"
    protocol                   = "Tcp"
    source_port_range          = "*"
    destination_port_range     = "22"
    source_address_prefix      = "Internet"
    destination_address_prefix = "*"
  }

  security_rule {
    name                       = "Allow-HTTP"
    description                = "Allow HTTP"
    priority                   = 110
    direction                  = "Inbound"
```

```
      access                  = "Allow"
      protocol                = "Tcp"
      source_port_range       = "*"
      destination_port_range  = "80"
      source_address_prefix   = "Internet"
      destination_address_prefix = "*"
  }
}

# Associate the web NSG with the subnet
resource "azurerm_subnet_network_security_group_association" "ngx-nsg-assoc" {
  depends_on=[azurerm_resource_group.network-rg]

  subnet_id                 = azurerm_subnet.vm-subnet.id
  network_security_group_id = azurerm_network_security_group.nginx-vm-nsg.id
}
```

# Deploying NGINX OSS in Debian and Ubuntu Linux

In this section, we are going to learn how to deploy a virtual machine with NGINX OSS running Ubuntu Linux. This code will work without major changes on Debian; we would just need to update the `source_image_reference` section (instructions are at the end of this chapter).

If you are using CentOS or Red Hat, please jump ahead to "Deploying NGINX OSS in CentOS and Red Hat Linux" on page 41.

### Bootstrapping script to install NGINX OSS

In this step, we will create a Bash script called *install-nginx.sh* to install NGINX OSS in the virtual machine:

```
#! /bin/bash
echo \
 "deb http://nginx.org/packages/mainline/ubuntu/ xenial nginx" \
 > /etc/apt/sources.list.d/nginx.list
echo \
 "deb-src http://nginx.org/packages/mainline/ubuntu/ xenial nginx" \
 >> /etc/apt/sources.list.d/nginx.list
wget http://nginx.org/keys/nginx_signing.key
apt-key add nginx_signing.key
apt-get update
apt-get -y install nginx

# Test NGINX is installed
nginx -v

# Start NGINX - it's enabled to start at boot by default
/etc/init.d/nginx start
```

## Creating the virtual machine

Here we will create a file called *vm-nginx-main.tf*. This file will load the bootstrapping script, get a public IP address, and create a virtual machine:

```
# Bootstrapping Template File
data "template_file" "nginx-vm-cloud-init" {
  template = file("install-nginx.sh")
}

# Generate random password
resource "random_password" "nginx-vm-password" {
  length          = 16
  min_upper       = 2
  min_lower       = 2
  min_special     = 2
  number          = true
  special         = true
  override_special = "!@#$%&"
}

# Get a Static Public IP
resource "azurerm_public_ip" "nginx-vm-ip" {
  depends_on=[azurerm_resource_group.network-rg]

  name                = "nginxvm-ip"
  location            = azurerm_resource_group.network-rg.location
  resource_group_name = azurerm_resource_group.network-rg.name
  allocation_method   = "Static"
}

# Create Network Card for the VM
resource "azurerm_network_interface" "nginx-nic" {
  depends_on=[azurerm_resource_group.network-rg]

  name                = "nginxvm-nic"
  location            = azurerm_resource_group.network-rg.location
  resource_group_name = azurerm_resource_group.network-rg.name

  ip_configuration {
    name                          = "internal"
    subnet_id                     = azurerm_subnet.vm-subnet.id
    private_ip_address_allocation = "Dynamic"
    public_ip_address_id          = azurerm_public_ip.nginx-vm-ip.id
  }
}

# Create NGINX VM
resource "azurerm_linux_virtual_machine" "nginx-vm" {
  depends_on=[azurerm_network_interface.nginx-nic]

  name                = "nginxvm"
  location            = azurerm_resource_group.network-rg.location
```

```
  resource_group_name   = azurerm_resource_group.network-rg.name
  network_interface_ids = [azurerm_network_interface.nginx-nic.id]
  size                  = var.nginx_vm_size

  source_image_reference {
    publisher = "Canonical"
    offer     = "UbuntuServer"
    sku       = "18.04-LTS"
    version   = "latest"
  }

  os_disk {
    name                 = "nginxvm-osdisk"
    caching              = "ReadWrite"
    storage_account_type = "Standard_LRS"
  }

  computer_name  = "nginxvm"
  admin_username = var.nginx_admin_username
  admin_password = random_password.nginx-vm-password.result
  custom_data    = base64encode(data.template_file.nginx-vm-cloud-init.rendered)

  disable_password_authentication = false
}
```

Then we create a file called *vm-nginx-variables.tf* to manage variables for virtual machines:

```
variable "nginx_vm_size" {
  type        = string
  description = "Size (SKU) of the virtual machine to create"
}

variable "nginx_admin_username" {
  description = "Username for Virtual Machine administrator account"
  type        = string
  default     = ""
}

variable "nginx_admin_password" {
  description = "Password for Virtual Machine administrator account"
  type        = string
  default     = ""
}
```

## Deploying NGINX OSS in CentOS and Red Hat Linux

In this section, we will deploy a virtual machine with NGINX OSS running CentOS Linux. If you prefer Ubuntu, you can skip these next two sections, as they overwrite the files created previously. This code will work on a Red Hat system without major changes; we would just need to update the NGINX OSS package repository, replacing centos with rhel, and the source_image_reference section in the *vm-nginx-main.tf* file.

### Bootstrapping script to install NGINX OSS

In this step, we overwrite the Bash script used in the previous Ubuntu section to install NGINX OSS through yum during the bootstrapping of the virtual machine. Replace the *install-nginx.sh* file with the following:

```
#! /bin/bash
echo "[nginx]
name=nginx repo
baseurl=http://nginx.org/packages/mainline/centos/7/$basearch/
gpgcheck=0
enabled=1" > /etc/yum.repos.d/nginx.repo

yum -y install nginx
systemctl enable nginx
systemctl start nginx
firewall-cmd --permanent --zone=public --add-port=80/tcp
firewall-cmd --reload
```

### Creating the virtual machine

Here we replace the file called *vm-nginx-main.tf*. This file will load the bootstrapping script, get a public IP address, and create a CentOS-based virtual machine that runs the bash shell at boot:

```
# Bootstrapping Template File
data "template_file" "nginx-vm-cloud-init" {
  template = file("install-nginx.sh")
}

# Generate random password
resource "random_password" "nginx-vm-password" {
  length          = 16
  min_upper       = 2
  min_lower       = 2
  min_special     = 2
  number          = true
  special         = true
  override_special = "!@#$%&"
}

# Get a Static Public IP
resource "azurerm_public_ip" "nginx-vm-ip" {
  depends_on=[azurerm_resource_group.network-rg]

  name                = "nginxvm-ip"
  location            = azurerm_resource_group.network-rg.location
  resource_group_name = azurerm_resource_group.network-rg.name
```

```
  allocation_method    = "Static"
}

# Create Network Card for the VM
resource "azurerm_network_interface" "nginx-nic" {
  depends_on=[azurerm_resource_group.network-rg]

  name                = "nginxvm-nic"
  location            = azurerm_resource_group.network-rg.location
  resource_group_name = azurerm_resource_group.network-rg.name

  ip_configuration {
    name                          = "internal"
    subnet_id                     = azurerm_subnet.vm-subnet.id
    private_ip_address_allocation = "Dynamic"
    public_ip_address_id          = azurerm_public_ip.nginx-vm-ip.id
  }
}

# Create NGINX VM
resource "azurerm_linux_virtual_machine" "nginx-vm" {
  depends_on=[azurerm_network_interface.nginx-nic]

  name                  = "nginxvm"
  location              = azurerm_resource_group.network-rg.location
  resource_group_name   = azurerm_resource_group.network-rg.name
  network_interface_ids = [azurerm_network_interface.nginx-nic.id]
  size                  = var.nginx_vm_size

  source_image_reference {
    publisher = "OpenLogic"
    offer     = "CentOS"
    sku       = "7_8-gen2"
    version   = "latest"
  }

  os_disk {
    name                 = "nginxvm-osdisk"
    caching              = "ReadWrite"
    storage_account_type = "Standard_LRS"
  }

  computer_name   = "nginxvm"
  admin_username  = var.nginx_admin_username
  admin_password  = random_password.nginx-vm-password.result
  custom_data     = base64encode(data.template_file.nginx-vm-cloud-init.rendered)

  disable_password_authentication = false
}
```

## Creating the input variables file

We can provide values to our variables through the *terraform.tfvars* file, or exported environment variables. This will make calling the `terraform` command line tool simpler.

Here are the PowerShell environment variables:

```
$Env:TF_VAR_location = "eastus"
$Env:TF_VAR_network-vnet-cidr = "10.0.0.0/24"
$Env:TF_VAR_vm-subnet-cidr    = "10.0.0.0/26"

$Env:TF_VAR_nginx_vm_size        = "Standard_B1s"
$Env:TF_VAR_nginx_admin_username = "admin"

$Env:TF_VAR_azure-subscription-id = "complete-here"
$Env:TF_VAR_azure-client-id       = "complete-here"
$Env:TF_VAR_azure-client-secret   = "complete-here"
$Env:TF_VAR_azure-tenant-id       = "complete-here"
```

And here are the Bash environment variables:

```
export TF_VAR_location = "eastus"
export TF_VAR_network-vnet-cidr = "10.0.0.0/24"
export TF_VAR_vm-subnet-cidr    = "10.0.0.0/26"

export TF_VAR_nginx_vm_size        = "Standard_B1s"
export TF_VAR_nginx_admin_username = "admin"

export TF_VAR_azure-subscription-id = "complete-here"
export TF_VAR_azure-client-id       = "complete-here"
export TF_VAR_azure-client-secret   = "complete-here"
export TF_VAR_azure-tenant-id       = "complete-here"
```

When using a *terraform.tsars*, ensure you never commit the file to source control or share the file with others:

```
location           = "eastus"
network-vnet-cidr = "10.0.0.0/24"
vm-subnet-cidr    = "10.0.0.0/26"

nginx_vm_size        = "Standard_B1s"
nginx_admin_username = "tfadmin"

azure-subscription-id = "complete-here"
azure-client-id       = "complete-here"
azure-client-secret   = "complete-here"
azure-tenant-id       = "complete-here"
```

# Running Terraform

We must first initialize our working directory for deploying Terraform:

```
terraform init
```

Before we run `terraform` to deploy our infrastructure, it's a good idea to use the `plan` command to discover what Terraform intends on doing in our Azure account:

```
terraform plan
```

If you approve the plan, you can apply the Terraform to your Azure account by running the following; when you are prompted to approve, type **yes**:

```
terraform apply
```

After Terraform runs, you can go find your newly created resources in Azure and use the IP address to view the default NGINX OSS landing page.

# Installing NGINX Plus via Terraform

In this section, we will deploy a Linux virtual machine with NGINX Plus using Terraform. Unlike the open source version, in this section we will deploy a virtual machine image preinstalled with NGINX Plus from the Azure Marketplace. Currently, NGINX Plus suggested Azure VM sizes are:

- Standard_A1
- Standard_A2
- Standard_A3

Before we get started with Terraform, we need to accept the Azure Marketplace terms using the following PowerShell script:

```
Get-AzMarketplaceTerms -Publisher "nginxinc" -Product "nginx-plus-v1" `
  -Name "nginx-plus-ub1804" | Set-AzMarketplaceTerms -Accept
```

### How to find Azure NGINX Plus VM images for Terraform using PowerShell

To deploy an NGINX Plus virtual machine, we will need to find the value for the `Publisher`, `offer`, and `sku` parameters of the Azure Marketplace source image, using PowerShell.

Start by defining the Azure region you'd like to provision into using a variable:

```
$Location = "East US"
```

Then set the a variable to hold the name of the publisher and query the list of offers. For NGINX Plus images, the publisher is called `nginxinc`:

```
$publisher = "nginxinc"
Get-AzVMImageOffer -Location $location -PublisherName $publisher | Select Offer
```

These are the results:

```
Offer
-----
nginx-plus-ent-v1
nginx-plus-v1
```

Next, we list SKUs for NGINX Plus. We do not want the enterprise agreement because that requires us to bring our own license. We'll instead use the standard offering to pay for the software license by the hour:

```
$offer = "nginx-plus-v1"
Get-AzVMImageSku -Location $location -PublisherName $publisher -Offer $offer | `
    Select Skus
```

These are the resulting SKUs:

```
Skus
----
nginx-plus-centos7
nginx-plus-q1fy17
nginx-plus-rhel7
nginx-plus-rhel8
nginx-plus-ub1604
nginx-plus-ub1804
```

As we can see, there are several options for an operating system to deploy NGINX Plus on Azure: CentOS Linux 7, Red Hat Enterprise Linux 7 and 8, and Ubuntu Linux 16.04 and 18.04.

If we want to use the enterprise version of NGINX Plus, we can use the following code to list SKUs:

```
$offer = "nginx-plus-ent-v1"
Get-AzVMImageSku -Location $location -PublisherName $publisher -Offer $offer | `
    Select Skus
```

The result will be as follows:

```
Skus
----
nginx-plus-ent-centos7
nginx-plus-ent-rhel7
nginx-plus-ent-ub1804
```

## The provider

The first step is to create the provider file for Terraform. The provider is used to interact with APIs.

We create a file called *provider-main.tf* that is used to create the interaction with Terraform and Azure providers:

```
# Define Terraform provider
terraform {
  required_version = ">= 0.12"
}

# Configure the Azure provider
provider "azurerm" {
  environment = "public"
  version     = ">= 2.15.0"
  features {}
  # It is important that the following values of these variables
  #  NEVER be written to source control, and therefore should not be
  #  hard-coded with defaults and should always come from the local
  #  environment
  subscription_id = var.azure-subscription-id
  client_id       = var.azure-client-id
  client_secret   = var.azure-client-secret
  tenant_id       = var.azure-tenant-id
}
```

Next, we create a file called *provider-variables.tf* that is used to manage the authentication variables of the Azure provider:

```
variable "azure-subscription-id" {
  type        = string
  description = "Azure Subscription ID"
}

variable "azure-client-id" {
  type        = string
  description = "Azure Client ID"
}

variable "azure-client-secret" {
  type        = string
  description = "Azure Client Secret"
}

variable "azure-tenant-id" {
  type        = string
  description = "Azure Tenant ID"
}
```

## The network

The next step is to create the resource group that will host all of our Azure resources. A VNET, and a subnet within the VNET, will also be created. The subnet will host our virtual machine.

We create a file called *network-main.tf* to describe these resources:

```
# Create a resource group
resource "azurerm_resource_group" "network-rg" {
  name     = "nginx-network-rg"
  location = var.location
}

# Create the network VNET
resource "azurerm_virtual_network" "network-vnet" {
  name                = "nginx-network-vnet"
  address_space       = [var.network-vnet-cidr]
  resource_group_name = azurerm_resource_group.network-rg.name
  location            = azurerm_resource_group.network-rg.location
}

# Create a subnet for VM
resource "azurerm_subnet" "vm-subnet" {
  name                 = "nginx-vm-subnet"
  address_prefixes     = [var.vm-subnet-cidr]
  virtual_network_name = azurerm_virtual_network.network-vnet.name
  resource_group_name  = azurerm_resource_group.network-rg.name
}
```

Then, we create the file *network-variables.tf* to manage network variables:

```
variable "location" {
  type        = string
  description = "Azure Region"
  default     = "eastus"
}

variable "network-vnet-cidr" {
  type        = string
  description = "The CIDR of the network VNET"
}

variable "vm-subnet-cidr" {
  type        = string
  description = "The CIDR for the vm subnet"
}
```

## Security

In this section, we will create an Azure NSG (network security group) to protect our virtual machine. The security group will allow inbound traffic in ports 22 (SSH), 80 (HTTP), and 443 (HTTPS).

---

**Opening SSH to the Internet**

For brevity, the following code will allow SSH connections from anywhere on the internet. You should determine your own needs for SSH access and restrict access accordingly.

We create a file called *security-main.tf* and add the following code:

```
# Create Network Security Group
resource "azurerm_network_security_group" "nginx-vm-nsg" {
  depends_on=[azurerm_resource_group.network-rg]

  name                = "nginxvm-nsg"
  location            = azurerm_resource_group.network-rg.location
  resource_group_name = azurerm_resource_group.network-rg.name

  security_rule {
    name                       = "Allow-SSH"
    description                = "Allow SSH"
    priority                   = 100
    direction                  = "Inbound"
    access                     = "Allow"
    protocol                   = "Tcp"
    source_port_range          = "*"
    destination_port_range     = "22"
    source_address_prefix      = "Internet"
    destination_address_prefix = "*"
  }

  security_rule {
    name                       = "Allow-HTTP"
    description                = "Allow HTTP"
    priority                   = 110
    direction                  = "Inbound"
    access                     = "Allow"
    protocol                   = "Tcp"
    source_port_range          = "*"
    destination_port_range     = "80"
    source_address_prefix      = "Internet"
    destination_address_prefix = "*"
  }

  security_rule {
    name                       = "Allow-HTTPS"
    description                = "Allow HTTPS"
    priority                   = 120
    direction                  = "Inbound"
    access                     = "Allow"
    protocol                   = "Tcp"
    source_port_range          = "*"
    destination_port_range     = "443"
    source_address_prefix      = "Internet"
```

```
      destination_address_prefix = "*"
    }
  }

  # Associate the web NSG with the subnet
  resource "azurerm_subnet_network_security_group_association" "ngx-nsg-assoc" {
    depends_on=[azurerm_resource_group.network-rg]

    subnet_id                 = azurerm_subnet.vm-subnet.id
    network_security_group_id = azurerm_network_security_group.nginx-vm-nsg.id
  }
```

### Define an NGINX Plus virtual machine

In this section, we will define a virtual machine with NGINX Plus.

First, we create a file called *vm-nginx-main.tf* and add code to generate a random password and a random virtual machine name:

```
# Generate random password.
resource "random_password" "nginx-vm-password" {
  length          = 16
  min_upper       = 2
  min_lower       = 2
  min_special     = 2
  number          = true
  special         = true
  override_special = "!@#$%&"
}

# Generate a random vm name
resource "random_string" "nginx-vm-name" {
  length  = 8
  upper   = false
  number  = false
  lower   = true
  special = false
}
```

Then, to the same file, we add code to request a public IP address, generate a network card, and assign the public IP address to it:

```
# Get a Static Public IP
resource "azurerm_public_ip" "nginx-vm-ip" {
  depends_on=[azurerm_resource_group.network-rg]

  name                = "nginx-${random_string.nginx-vm-name.result}-ip"
  location            = azurerm_resource_group.network-rg.location
  resource_group_name = azurerm_resource_group.network-rg.name
  allocation_method   = "Static"
}

# Create Network Card for the VM
```

```
resource "azurerm_network_interface" "nginx-nic" {
  depends_on=[azurerm_resource_group.network-rg]

  name                = "nginx-${random_string.nginx-vm-name.result}-nic"
  location            = azurerm_resource_group.network-rg.location
  resource_group_name = azurerm_resource_group.network-rg.name

  ip_configuration {
    name                          = "internal"
    subnet_id                     = azurerm_subnet.vm-subnet.id
    private_ip_address_allocation = "Dynamic"
    public_ip_address_id          = azurerm_public_ip.nginx-vm-ip.id
  }
}
```

Next, we add the definition to create the virtual machine with the NGINX Plus:

```
# Create NGINX VM
resource "azurerm_linux_virtual_machine" "nginx-vm" {
  depends_on=[azurerm_network_interface.nginx-nic]

  name                = "nginx-${random_string.nginx-vm-name.result}-vm"
  location            = azurerm_resource_group.network-rg.location
  resource_group_name = azurerm_resource_group.network-rg.name
  network_interface_ids = [azurerm_network_interface.nginx-nic.id]
  size                = var.nginx_vm_size

  source_image_reference {
    publisher = var.nginx-publisher
    offer     = var.nginx-plus-offer
    sku       = "nginx-plus-ub1804"
    version   = "latest"
  }

  plan {
    name      = "nginx-plus-ub1804"
    publisher = var.nginx-publisher
    product   = var.nginx-plus-offer
  }

  os_disk {
    name                 = "nginx-${random_string.nginx-vm-name.result}-osdisk"
    caching              = "ReadWrite"
    storage_account_type = "Standard_LRS"
  }

  computer_name  = "nginx-${random_string.nginx-vm-name.result}-vm"
  admin_username = var.nginx_admin_username
  admin_password = random_password.nginx-vm-password.result

  disable_password_authentication = false
}
```

Finally, we create a file called *vm-nginx-variables.tf* to manage variables for virtual machines:

```
variable "nginx_vm_size" {
  type        = string
  description = "Size (SKU) of the virtual machine to create"
}

variable "nginx_admin_username" {
  description = "Username for Virtual Machine administrator account"
  type        = string
  default     = ""
}

variable "nginx_admin_password" {
  description = "Password for Virtual Machine administrator account"
  type        = string
  default     = ""
}

variable "nginx-publisher" {
  type        = string
  description = "Publisher ID for NGINX"
  default     = "nginxinc"
}

variable "nginx-plus-offer" {
  type        = string
  description = "Offer ID for NGINX"
  default     = "nginx-plus-v1"
}
```

### Creating the input variables file

We can provide values to our variables through the *terraform.tfvars* file, or exported environment variables; this will make calling the `terraform` command line tool simpler.

Here are the PowerShell environment variables:

```
$Env:TF_VAR_location = "eastus"
$Env:TF_VAR_network-vnet-cidr = "10.0.0.0/24"
$Env:TF_VAR_vm-subnet-cidr    = "10.0.0.0/26"

$Env:TF_VAR_nginx_vm_size       = "Standard_B1s"
$Env:TF_VAR_nginx_admin_username = "admin"

$Env:TF_VAR_azure-subscription-id = "complete-here"
$Env:TF_VAR_azure-client-id       = "complete-here"
$Env:TF_VAR_azure-client-secret   = "complete-here"
$Env:TF_VAR_azure-tenant-id       = "complete-here"
```

And here are the Bash environment variables:

```
export TF_VAR_location = "eastus"
export TF_VAR_network-vnet-cidr = "10.0.0.0/24"
export TF_VAR_vm-subnet-cidr    = "10.0.0.0/26"

export TF_VAR_nginx_vm_size        = "Standard_B1s"
export TF_VAR_nginx_admin_username = "admin"

export TF_VAR_azure-subscription-id = "complete-here"
export TF_VAR_azure-client-id       = "complete-here"
export TF_VAR_azure-client-secret   = "complete-here"
export TF_VAR_azure-tenant-id       = "complete-here"
```

When using a *terraform.tsars*, ensure you never commit the file to source control or share the file with others:

```
location          = "eastus"
network-vnet-cidr = "10.0.0.0/24"
vm-subnet-cidr    = "10.0.0.0/26"

nginx_vm_size        = "Standard_B1s"
nginx_admin_username = "admin"

azure-subscription-id = "complete-here"
azure-client-id       = "complete-here"
azure-client-secret   = "complete-here"
azure-tenant-id       = "complete-here"
```

## Running Terraform

Before we run `terraform`, it's a good idea to use the `plan` command to discover what Terraform intends on doing in our Azure account:

```
terraform plan
```

If you approve the plan, you can apply the Terraform to your Azure account by running the following. When you are prompted to approve, type **yes**:

```
terraform apply
```

After Terraform runs, you can go find your newly created resources in Azure and use the IP address to view the default NGINX Plus landing page.

## Conclusion

This chapter was a chance to deploy both NGINX OSS and NGINX Plus and to explore the levels of functionality available from both products, as well as the differences between them. NGINX OSS is free but requires a better understanding of how to deploy it and how to make the best use of its feature set. NGINX Plus has several varied and convenient options for deployment and is a commercial product that offers advanced features and enterprise-level support as licensed software by NGINX, Inc.

We deployed NGINX OSS and NGINX Plus using a combination of the Azure Portal, PowerShell, and Terraform to see the available options. Terraform provided the most complete solution for NGINX OSS and NGINX Plus, allowing the greatest levels of automation and integration into a full Azure deployment scenario.

To learn in detail how to configure NGINX, consider checking out Derek's book, *NGINX Cookbook: Advanced Recipes for High-Performance Load Balancing* (O'Reilly).

In the next chapter, we will compare the features of Azure managed load-balancing solutions with NGINX and NGINX Plus.

# CHAPTER 4

# NGINX and Microsoft Managed Options

Microsoft Azure provides a number of different proxy-like, data plane–level services that forward a request or connection through different networking layers, load balancing and applying rules along the way. NGINX provides much of the same functionality as these services but can reside deeper in the stack, and it has less configuration limitation. When delivering applications hosted in Microsoft Azure, you need to determine what controls are needed where, and how best to provide them.

Most of the time the right answer is not one service or the other, but a mix. By layering proxy-like services in front of your application, you're able to maintain more control and distribute the incoming load. The Azure services are meant to complement one another by being layered throughout the stack. NGINX is interchangeable with the Azure services that reside in the Azure Virtual Network. A major added value of Azure managed services is that because they are managed, they do not require maintenance and care on your part.

The Azure managed services that provide proxy-like, data plane–level services are Azure Front Door, CDN Profiles, Application Gateway, and Load Balancer. All of them have valid use cases, some have overlapping features, and they all can be frontends for NGINX. Azure Front Door is covered in depth in Chapter 5; the present chapter will focus on Azure Load Balancer, the Application Gateway, and the integration with Azure WAF policies. CDN Profiles, while they do act as a proxy, are not designed for load balancing, therefore are not discussed in this book.

# Comparing NGINX and Azure Load Balancer

Azure Load Balancer operates at Layer 4 of the OSI model, the transport layer. This means that Azure Load Balancer is chauffeuring the connection from the client to a backend server. As the connection is direct between the client and the server, Azure Load Balancer is not considered a proxy. Only data within the connection headers is used or updated by Azure Load Balancer; it does not and cannot use or manipulate the data within the packets.

Using information from the connection headers, Azure Load Balancer can determine to which backend server it should route the request. Load balancing of a connection is performed by a hash algorithm that uses the connection headers to place a connection across the backend pool. Five pieces of information are used from the connection header to generate the hash:

- Source IP
- Source port
- Destination IP
- Destination port
- IP protocol

Azure Load Balancer calls the connection sessions *flows*, because a flow may consist of multiple connections. Because the source port usually changes between connections, Azure Load Balancer creates an affinity, or rudimentary session persistence, between client and server by hashing only a portion of the connection header information that is used for initial distribution. As a result, connections from a given source IP, destination IP, and destination port will be pinned to the same backend server.

This operating model is different from NGINX, because NGINX operates at Layer 7 of the OSI model, the application layer. With NGINX there are two connections: one between the client and NGINX and another between NGINX and the server. Acting as an intermediary in the connection makes NGINX a proxy.

Operating at Layer 7, NGINX has the ability to read and manipulate the data packet bound from the client to the server, and the response bound from the server to the client. In this way, NGINX can understand higher-level application protocols such as HTTP and use that information for routing, whereas Layer 4 load balancers just enable the transport of a connection.

# Use Cases

There are valid use cases for both. With Layer 4 load balancing, the direct connection between the client and the server has benefits. The server receives the direct connection and has all of the original connection information without having to understand proxy protocol. This is especially important for legacy applications that depend on a direct connection with the client. A proxy scenario also has its benefits, as it's able to control the backend connections and therefore can optimize or manipulate those in any way it may need to. If an application relies on client information in the connection headers, it would simply need to understand the proxy protocol. The proxy protocol appends information about proxies the request has passed through on its way to the server. The proxy protocol is an addendum to Layer 7 protocols, which means the information goes in the application layer protocol headers and not in the connection headers.

Despite these differences, the two solutions have things in common. Both NGINX and Azure Load Balancer are able to load balance traffic and can route based on connection information. Both are able to listen for incoming traffic on one port and direct the request to the backend service, which may be on a different port; in the Layer 4 scenario this is considered Network Address Translation, or NAT, whereas in a proxy scenario this doesn't have a name—it's just part of the nature of creating the second connection. Both Azure Load Balancer and NGINX can perform TCP and UDP load balancing.

While the solutions are different from each other and serve their own use cases, it's not uncommon to see them working together. Azure Load Balancer complements NGINX well when multiple NGINX machines are deployed and the traffic bound for them needs to be balanced with something more sophisticated than DNS. Don't be surprised to see Azure Load Balancer in front of a fleet of NGINX nodes.

# Comparing NGINX and Azure Application Gateway Functionality

Where Azure Load Balancer and NGINX differ, Azure Application Gateway and NGINX have more commonalities. Azure Application Gateway operates at Layer 7, like NGINX. To operate at this layer, Azure Application Gateway must and does act as a proxy. One major difference is that NGINX is able to do this for all TCP and UDP protocols, whereas Application Gateway is concentrated only on HTTP(S).

By receiving the request and understanding the HTTP protocol, Application Gateway is able to use HTTP header information to make decisions about how to route or respond to requests. The idea of an Application Gateway, or API gateway, is to consolidate multiple microservices that make up a service or product offering under a single API endpoint. This API endpoint understands the services that it's providing for, as well as its overall API spec.

**Concept Versus Product Terminology**

In the following sections, we will use the term *API gateway* to refer to a concept that Azure Application Gateway, NGINX, and other application delivery controllers all fit into. When referring to the product Azure Application Gateway, we'll use the term *Azure Application Gateway* or *Application Gateway*.

By having a full understanding of the API spec, an API gateway can validate requests on their way to your application. If a request is invalid, it can be denied at the API gateway. Basic matching of requests for redirection is also possible. The power and necessity of an API gateway lie in its ability to route traffic to different backend services based on the URI path. Microservices for RESTful APIs are typically broken up by the sets of API resources they handle, and that's reflected by the API's path. In this way, we can use URI path matching to direct requests for specific API resources, based on information in the URI, to the correct microservices.

An example of URI-based routing would be if we had two services, authentication and users. Our API gateway handles requests for both but routes each request based on the URI. Resource requests for authentication are behind a URI path prefix of */auth/*, and requests for the users service are behind a URI path prefix of */users/*. Figure 4-1 depicts this scenario.

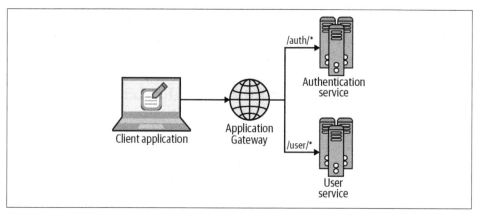

*Figure 4-1. URI-based routing with Azure Application Gateway.*

Once the API gateway has validated a request and matched a URI path routing rule, it can manipulate the request it makes to the backend service by altering headers, or URI paths. It can perform these actions because it is a proxy and is making its own connection and requests to the backend service on behalf of the request it received from the client. This is important to note because you may have headers that are used only internally, or paths on the backend services may not match exactly what your frontend API provides. By virtue of being a proxy, the API gateway is also able to terminate SSL/TLS, meaning that connections to backend services may not be encrypted, or use a different certificate for that connection.

Once the request is ready to be sent to a backend service, the feature sets of what could be considered an API gateway versus what more advanced data plane services provide start to differ. Both Azure Application Gateway and NGINX are able to provide load balancing, whereas some API gateways would simply pass the request to a load balancer. Having load balancing built into an API gateway solution is nice because it saves a hop in the connection and provides a complete control in between client-server communication and routing in a single system.

### Connection Draining

A useful feature that both Azure Application Gateway and NGINX Plus provide is connection draining, which allows live connections to finish before removing a backend node from the load-balancing pool. This feature is not available in the open source version of NGINX.

When load balancing requests, there is sometimes a need for session persistence. In Azure it's referred to as *session affinity*. When a backend service does not share session state between horizontally scaled nodes, subsequent requests need to be routed to the same backend node. The most common case of requiring session persistence is when legacy applications are ported to a cloud environment and session state has not yet moved off local disk or memory to storage that is network addressable, such as Redis or Memcached. This is less common with API gateways, as they were built around more modern-day web architecture. A scenario in which an API gateway may require session persistence might be when the session data being worked with is too large to be performant over the network.

An important feature that both NGINX and Azure Application Gateway provide is the support of Websockets and HTTP/2 traffic. HTTP/2 enables the client-server connection to pass multiple requests through a single connection, cutting down on handshakes and SSL/TLS negotiation. The server in the case of HTTP/2 is the API gateway. A Websocket enables bidirectional communication between the client and server over a long-standing connection. The server in this case is the backend application server.

A feature that NGINX provides but Azure Application Gateway does not is HTTP/2 push. HTTP/2 push is a feature of the HTTP/2 protocol in which the server can push extra documents that it knows are going to be subsequent requests. One common example would be in response to a request for *index.html*, where the server knows that the browser will also need some CSS and JavaScript documents. The server can push those documents with the response for *index.html* to save on round-trip requests.

Azure Application Gateway and NGINX are a lot alike; however, Azure Application Gateway is missing one important and welcome feature of an API gateway, which is the ability to validate authentication. The web has began to standardize on JSON Web Tokens, or JWTs, which use asymmetric encryption to validate identity claims. Standard authentication workflows such as OAUTH/2 and OpenId Connect utilize JWTs, which enables services that can validate JWTs to take part in the authentication validation process. NGINX Plus is able to validate JWTs out of the box, whereas with open source NGINX, validation requires a bit of work through extendable programming. Both NGINX and NGINX Plus can also perform authentication subrequests, where the request or a portion of the request can be sent to an authentication service for validation before NGINX proxies the request to a backend service. Azure Application Gateway does not offer any authentication validation, meaning your services will need to validate the request once it is received, whereas this action could and should be offloaded to the API gateway whenever possible.

# Comparing NGINX and Azure Web Application Firewall Capabilities

A Web Application Firewall (WAF) is a Layer 7 proxy that specifically reviews the request for security exploits and determines whether the request should be proxied to the backend service or denied. The request is evaluated against a number of rules that look for things like cross-site scripting, SQL injection, known bad bots, protocol violations, application language and framework-specific vulnerabilities, and size limit abuse. Azure services and NGINX are able to act as Web Application Firewalls.

Azure provides Web Application Firewall capabilities in the form of policies that can be attached to the Azure Front Door and Application Gateway services. Azure WAF policies comprise a number of rules. These rules take the form of managed rule sets provided by Azure and custom rules defined by you. Managed rule sets are supplied by Azure, and at least one must be configured. Individual rules within a managed rule set can be disabled if necessary. The managed rule sets provide protection out of the box, but you can also build and apply your own custom rules on top of the managed rule set. You can set specific custom WAF rules or entire policies to block or passively monitor and record events.

When using custom rules, you can match on a number of different conditions gleaned from the request. A rule is made up of numerous components, such as the type of match, where to find the variable, an operator, and our matching pattern.

The following describes the types of rules that can be set up and their different options:

*IP address*
> The source IP address of the request is matched inclusively or exclusively against a CIDR range, or specific IP address.

*Number*
> A variable numeric value that is derived from the query string, request URI, headers, arguments, body, or cookies and that is or is not less than, greater to, or equal to a specific value.

*String*
> A variable string value that is derived from the query string, request URI, headers, arguments, body, or cookies. The value is evaluated by an operator to determine whether the derived string contains, begins with, ends with, or is equal to the value of the string provided in the rule.

*Geo location*
> The variable derived from the source IP or request header is compared against an array of country or region codes. The rule allows the provided country or region code list to be inclusive or exclusive.

Azure WAF policies log and produce a metric for each blocked request. The log has metadata about the request and the rule that blocked it. The metric can be filtered by rule name and action type. Metrics can be found in Azure Monitor. Logs are able to be streamed to an Azure Storage Account, Event Hub, or Log Analytics. This monitoring information allows you to analyze how your WAF rules are performing and whether they're flagging false positives. With any WAF you should monitor live traffic with your rule set in a mode that passively monitors for rule violations, review the information, and confirm that the WAF is working appropriately before enabling it to actively block traffic.

The Azure WAF policies are a great addition to the Azure managed service offerings. WAF policies should be enabled at any layer of your Azure environment to which they can be applied. Being that these are fully managed and come with default rule sets, there's no reason not to take advantage of them.

## ModSecurity

The aforementioned functionality provides the basis for what would be considered a WAF: evaluating requests to block based on matching rules. These rules can be configured to be extremely versatile and specific to block all sorts of attacks. This type of functionality can be found in the open source Web Application Firewall ModSecurity, which integrates directly into NGINX. ModSecurity is a rule engine specifically for matching web request attributes.

Installing ModSecurity for NGINX provides the same type of plug-in option as the Azure WAF policies do for Application Gateway. With ModSecurity, you can find a number of community-maintained rule sets ready for use, plug them in, and get going. ModSecurity's configuration capabilities go extremely deep, such that entire books have been written on the topic. One of the most popular community-maintained rule sets is the OWASP ModSecurity Core Rule Set (CRS), which is provided by the OWASP project. The OWASP CRS is one of the two managed rule sets provided by Azure WAF policies; the other is a list specifically about bots. The OWASP CRS is versioned, and at the time of writing, the latest public rule set version is 3.2, while the latest offered by Azure is 3.1.

Another extremely popular rule set is from Trustwave SpiderLabs. It requires a commercial subscription but is updated daily, so your ModSecurity rules are always up to date on the most recently discovered vulnerabilities and web attack patterns. The increased rate of updates on current web attacks is worth a premium over waiting for Azure to update its managed rule sets.

If you are comparing these two options, you're weighing a fully managed solution against a DIY open source solution. There are clear pros and cons here. Being fully managed with simplified configuration is a clear pro for Azure WAF policies. Bleeding-edge updates to security patterns and advanced configuration are a clear win for NGINX with ModSecurity. The cons are the exact reverse of the pros: NGINX must be managed by you and is more complicated to configure, whereas Azure is not bleeding edge on security updates but is easy to configure and doesn't require management on your part. This, however, does not have to be an either/or comparison. You can use a mix of the two, applying Azure WAF polices to Azure Front Door and using NGINX as a WAF at the API gateway layer. A determination of what is best for your situation will depend on circumstantial conditions within your organization.

# NGINX App Protect

After F5 acquired NGINX, it integrated the F5 WAF with NGINX Plus to create a commercial WAF option for NGINX Plus called the NGINX App Protect module. The App Protect module is more advanced than ModSecurity and receives updated signatures from F5 to keep the rules up to date with the latest security policies.

To use NGINX App Protect, you need a subscription to NGINX Plus and a subscription to NGINX App Protect. You can subscribe through the marketplace (NGINX Plus with NGINX App Protect) or the installation is done through a private NGINX Plus repository for the package manager being used by your system. After the module is installed, it can be dynamically loaded into NGINX Plus, enabled, and provided with a policy file. A passive mode can be enabled by turning on the module's logging directive and providing a log location. The log location consists of a JSON configuration file and a destination. The destination may be the local or remote syslog receiver, a file, or /dev/stderr. The JSON configuration file enables filtering of which events are logged. An example follows:

```
{
    "filter":{
        "request_type":"all"
    },
    "content":{
        "format":"default",
        "max_request_size":"any",
        "max_message_size":"5k"
    }
}
```

As mentioned before, it is recommended that you monitor a rule set before enabling it to understand the pattern of what will be blocked or allowed.

Once logging is set up, the App Protect module is open to a vast amount of configuration through the policy file. NGINX and F5 have provided a number of different templates to enable you to protect your apps with high-level definitions rather than building your own rules, though that is an option. Each policy provides the ability to set an enforcementMode attribute to transparent or blocking. This is an advantage over turning the entire WAF on or off because you can test certain policies while still enforcing those policies you know are good.

The attribute names of a policy file speak for themselves. The following is an example of a policy:

```
{
    "policy": {
        "name": "blocking_policy",
        "template": { "name": "POLICY_TEMPLATE_NGINX_BASE" },
        "applicationLanguage": "utf-8",
        "enforcementMode": "blocking",
        "blocking-settings": {
            "violations": [
                {
                    "name": "VIOL_JSON_FORMAT",
                    "alarm": true,
                    "block": true
                },
                {
                    "name": "VIOL_PARAMETER_VALUE_META CHAR",
                    "alarm": true,
                    "block": false
                }
            ]
        }
```

```
      }
  }
```

At its core, App Protect is still using the same information from requests to look for malicious requests based on a number of filters, but the funding behind it has enabled it to advance past what's going on in the open source WAF options. One of the most valuable features of the App Protect module is its ability to filter responses, which enables us to filter outbound data to prevent sensitive data from leaving the system. Credit card information is an example of data that should never be returned to the user, and with the ability to filter responses, we can ensure that it doesn't. When dealing with sensitive information, risk reduction of data leaks is of the highest importance.

App Protect is, in a way, a managed service because of the updated signatures and the number of high-level features. Prebuilt parsers for application data transfer standards like JSON and XML, SQL and Mogno syntaxes, and Linux and Windows Commands enable higher-level controls. Signature updates take a load of security management responsibility off an organization. It takes a certain degree of skill and effort to build complex filter rules to block only bad requests while staying up to date with the landscape of active new threats.

NGINX Plus with the App Protect module flips the management versus configurability scenario. The rules are tightly managed by the subscription, and the configuration options are more in-depth, but you have to manage the hosting and underlying OS. Hosting and ensuring availability is par for the course in cloud environments, and thus if you build and configure your NGINX Plus layer as you do your application code, it's no more than another app on the stack. This makes a solid case for distributing your data plane technologies; by layering *fully managed* with *highly configurable* and *up to date*, you build toward the highest levels of security and availability.

# Highly Available Multiregion NGINX Plus with Traffic Manager

Now that you have an understanding of how managed Azure load-balancing solutions and NGINX compare, we'll take a look at how you can layer solutions to enhance your web application offering.

All of the same concepts apply when using NGINX as a load balancer or API gateway over the Azure managed offerings. Because of distribution and point of presence locations that Azure managed services provide, you should utilize the global managed services from Azure to distribute load and route client requests to the correct environment region.

Figure 4-2 shows a multiregion deployment using NGINX Plus as an API gateway in both regions. NGINX Plus is also being used to load balance over a database tier. Traffic is routed through Traffic Manager using the Performance algorithm to provide clients with responses from the least latent region.

The Content Delivery Network, if the request is not cached, will proxy the request to the nearest region, where the request will be received by NGINX Plus. NGINX Plus will decrypt the request in the case of HTTPS. NGINX Plus inspects the request and routes to different server pools based on the request URI. The backend service may make a request through another NGINX Plus load-balancing tier to access the database.

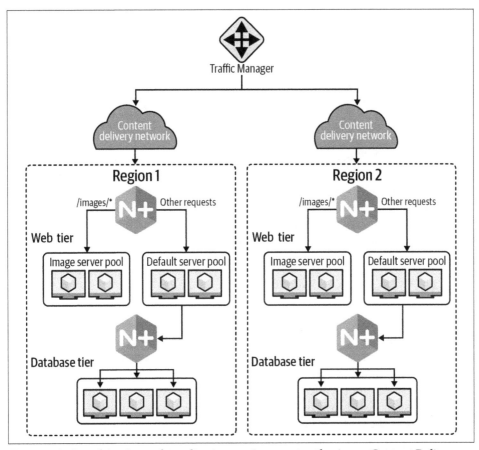

*Figure 4-2. A multiregion web application on Azure using the Azure Content Delivery Network, which uses Traffic Manager to route the client's request to the point of presence closest to the user.*

Figure 4-3 depicts a scenario in which Traffic Manager uses geography-based routing to direct a client in California to the US-West Azure region based on the user's geography. A client in California makes a DNS request, and Traffic Manager responds with the endpoint for US-West. The client makes a direct connection to NGINX Plus in the US-West region. NGINX Plus then decrypts the request in the case of HTTPS. NGINX Plus inspects the request and routes the request based on its own rules and proxies the request, which may be reencrypted.

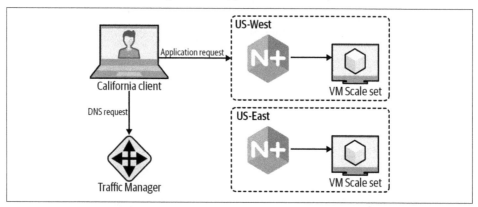

*Figure 4-3. NGINX Plus, along with GeoDNS, enables a globally distributed application.*

In these scenarios, Traffic Manager is directing our client to an available region that best fits the client's needs or the needs of our regulation. NGINX Plus is providing the API gateway functionality, as well as internal load balancing. These solutions together enable high availability failover, as well as highly configurable traffic routing within our environment.

# Conclusion

Microsoft Azure provides a number of different data plane managed services to aid in stronger and more reliable delivery of your application. Throughout this chapter, you learned how Azure Load Balancer, Application Gateway, and WAF Policies work, how they differ, and how they can be used with NGINX or NGINX Plus. The knowledge of where these different services fit in the stack enables you to make informed architecture decisions about load balancing and application delivery for your cloud platform and about the trade-off between functionality and management.

In this chapter we introduced the idea of layering Microsoft Azure managed load balancing solutions with NGINX. In the next chapter, we will add another layer to the managed Azure data plane service by looking at the Azure Front Door service and at how it can be used with NGINX.

# CHAPTER 5

# Azure Front Door with NGINX

## What Is the Azure Front Door Service?

Azure Front Door is a service that provides global web traffic routing, optimized for performance and high availability failover. Front Door is useful in all types of scenarios, especially multiregional deployments. As the name implies, Front Door is meant to be the first and primary access point between your client and your web service. Front Door always answers your client with a local connection, and then works as an operator to connect the client to the closest available next hop for that request. By acting as a configurable distributed proxy, Front Door enables you to have Layer 7 routing and network control at the edge.

Front Door uses latency-based DNS routing to connect the client to the nearest Front Door POP, or point of presence. POP locations differ from regions in that there are more of them, and they are distributed to be closer to the user. Latency-based routing is used for the backend connection as well, routing client requests to the nearest installation to a given service, wherever in the world it may be. Being health aware, Front Door automatically enables multiregion failover. Backend pools can be constructed with a number of different Azure services and internet standard endpoints. What makes Azure Front Door special is that it is network-optimized by use of a split TCP-based anycast protocol.

### Split TCP

Split TCP is a technique aimed at reducing latency packet delivery issues by separating the TCP connections between client and backend. This has an impact on distant and dynamic mobile connections, optimizing at the TCP and TLS handshake layers by use of proximity to reduce network latency. The Front Door Service takes on the role of a proxy; the client's TCP connection to the Front Door is quick because of the network proximity of the Front Door POP. On the backend, Front Door can preestablish and reuse TCP connections. By reusing connections to secure backends, Front Door also reduces the amount of TCP and TLS negotiations that need to happen. The anycast aspect happens at the DNS level to determine the closest POP, as well as at the backend to determine the closest endpoint. This use of anycast connects global users to a healthy service with the least number of network hops, thereby lowering network latency.

## Front Door Features

Azure Front Door Service includes a number of other useful features you would want at the edge layer—caching and Web Application Firewall (WAF), for example. If a managed edge service can validate the request and respond to your client, the user experience is enhanced by the response time, and your business logic receives only valid, necessary requests. Better response times and less stress on your resources add up to a clear win-win for you and your clients.

Other Azure Front Door features, such as TLS termination, session persistence, redirects, and rewrites, are what you would expect of a proxy. In our experience in the industry, the term *TLS termination* is sometimes used to describe what we would consider necessary to Layer 7 routing. An application-aware router must decrypt the packet to operate on Layer 7. On the other hand, we and others use the term *TLS termination* to describe when a proxy receives a secure connection and then proxies the request over an insecure connection, effectively terminating the encryption. Both uses are acceptable; just make sure you know how the term is being used. Front Door must decrypt the request for it to route appropriately. Front Door may route the request to a secure or insecure endpoint upstream. If you have a number of backend pools that consist of varying TLS certificates and want to consolidate or extrapolate their frontend presence, Azure Front Door is a great choice.

In the event that backend services rely on session persistence and are incapable of sharing session data, Front Door can create a cookie for the client to bind it to a backend endpoint. Based on the client cookie, Front Door will continually route specific client requests to that same backend endpoint.

When using a redirect, Azure Front Door simply provides a 3xx-level HTTP response to the client for a given rule match. However, rewrites enable you to alter the request URI. If you're familiar with NGINX rewrites, Azure Front Door's rewrites are much simpler. In NGINX, the notion of a rewrite triggers reprocessing of the request through the proxy rules. A rewrite in Azure Front Door enables you to modify the requested URI path before making an upstream request to the backend pool endpoint. Think of a rewrite with Front Door as the functionality NGINX provides by allowing manipulation of the request URI before using the `proxy_pass` directive.

## Front Door's Place in the Stack

Azure Front Door can listen for multiple frontend configuration endpoints and directly respond with blocks, redirects, and cached content. Requests not served directly have routing rules applied to direct the request to the intended healthy backend service. Network optimization for latency happens by proximity and connection management. Request routing with Front Door is at the macro level, connecting frontend listeners with backend service providers by hostname or by URI path. Using Azure Front Door provides the usefulness of a proxy in close proximity to the client, which you can configure but do not have to actively manage. Figure 5-1 depicts how a client would connect to an application through Azure Front Door.

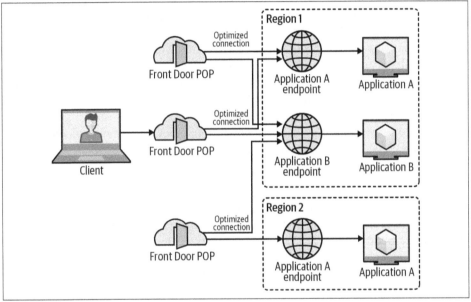

*Figure 5-1. The closest Front Door point of presence receives the client's request and then proxies it over an optimized connection to the closest application endpoint. One Front Door POP makes that connection across regions, because Application B does not exist in Region 2.*

# Benefits of Azure Front Door Service with NGINX

Azure Front Door and NGINX have a lot of overlapping functionality, but they complement each other by being at different layers of the stack. Front Door initially receives the request, doing high-level routing and optimization closest to the consumer before proxying requests to a more centralized location for more specific routing and load balancing.

Front Door's physical distribution adds a lot of benefits itself, but using Front Door with NGINX allows for further optimization. By knowing the way Front Door operates, NGINX can be optimized to keep client connections and TLS sessions open longer. Usually client connections and TLS sessions would be kept fairly low when serving directly to the end consumer to limit the memory and file-handling limitations of a server. In a scenario in which we do control the client, Front Door, we can lengthen the amount of time client connections are open to optimize connections safely. This optimization can also be made between NGINX and the upstream application server, as we have complete control over that client-server communication as well.

You may want to employ some of the overlapping functionality at a single layer. If you can offload processing or responses to a managed edge service, you should do so. Limiting the amount of processing for a given request will result in optimizing usage costs. When using Azure Front Door in conjunction with NGINX, focus your attention on content caching, macro-level routing, and regional failover at the edge, Front Door. Use NGINX as the reverse proxy load balancer at the micro level, routing between internal microservices that make up a service offering. In regards to blocking, security is done in layers, enabling Front Door WAF, along with NGINX working as a WAF, to provide a second layer of protection; this is an example of where overlapping functionality would be desired at both layers.

NGINX fits as the last layer between the public internet or other Azure services and your internal applications on the private network. In that regard, NGINX is much more intimate with the applications that make up the service offering and is prime for private communication between machines on the internal network. Whereas Azure provides the building's Front Door, NGINX acts as the office suite door. Once the request has entered the office, it's directed to a specific conference room or personal office for fulfillment. If a posted sign or a lock on the outside of a building does not meet the need, an office door or front desk attendant may; if not, only then will internal resources be utilized.

This sort of layering of application delivery controllers, or Layer 7 proxies, provides security, as well as thorough customization for web request routing.

# Integrating Azure Front Door Service with NGINX

To integrate Azure Front Door with NGINX, you need to configure NGINX as a backend pool to Front Door.

If you have not already done so, you'll need to build a Front Door. Using the Azure Console or some other infrastructure management tool, construct a Front Door configured for your subscription ID, resource group, and region. Next, configure a frontend host for Front Door by defining the hostname and enabling session affinity or

WAF if necessary. To utilize the WAF capabilities, you will need to have pre-existing Azure WAF policies.

## Front Door Features

Once you have a frontend host configured, you can set up a backend pool. You can add multiple backend pools to a Front Door, so if you already have a Front Door set up, you can add another backend pool for your NGINX backend.

Backends are logical; if a service is distributed regionally, each endpoint should be grouped and added to the same backend pool. In this manner, Front Door will enable failover and automatically route to the closest endpoint.

Add NGINX endpoints as backend hosts to a backend pool. The host header used when proxying the request to NGINX is configurable, which may be useful when the NGINX node receives requests for multiple domains and then routes appropriately, even if DNS for the hostname is not actually pointed at the NGINX endpoint but rather is pointed somewhere else, such as at Front Door. Configure any health probes that determine whether the nodes in the backend pool are healthy. Azure Front Door will direct requests only to backend pools that pass their health probes.

## Routing Rules

Next, apply routing rules to map the frontend host to the backend pool. In this section of the Front Door configuration, you can match based on the request URI and choose to redirect or forward the request. To route to NGINX, you would forward the request, at which point you can choose to rewrite it to manipulate its URI.

Once this section is configured and the Front Door is deployed, it is passing requests to NGINX.

## Optimizing with NGINX

To optimize NGINX for use with Azure Front Door Service, tune the length of time NGINX allows for client connections and TLS sessions. You can do so by use of the `keepalive_timeout` directive and the `ssl_session_timeout` directive. The default `keepalive_timeout` is 75 seconds, and the default `ssl_session_timeout` is 5 minutes:

```
server {
    # Your server configuration
    keepalive_timeout 300s;
    ssl_session_timeout 300s;
}
```

# Conclusion

In this chapter, you learned about the Azure Front Door Service and the optimizations it can provide for your application. Now that you have a full view of the services Azure provides for the data plane layer, you can start to see how the pieces fit together for your scenario. This layer of Azure managed service provides a way to distribute the endpoint connection for the client to the closest location to lower latency. Together with NGINX, Azure Front Door can handle the initial request, run it through initial managed WAF, and then proxy the request over an optimized connection to an NGINX API gateway for more control over delivery of your application.

# CHAPTER 6

# Monitoring NGINX in Microsoft Azure

Monitoring application performance is as important as monitoring your network, infrastructure, or security. Applications contain valuable data that you can use to fine-tune performance and function or prevent possible failures. Both Microsoft Azure and NGINX offer several tools and plug-ins for detailed application performance monitoring.

## Azure Monitor

Monitoring and understanding your application's performance and being able to identify and address any issues that may affect the application or its resources are necessary tasks. Azure Monitor collects data from your Azure environment for analysis and proactive planning.

Azure Monitor captures data from a variety of sources, such as the application, OS, or custom sources. The two primary data types, metrics and logs, are kept in data stores. Metrics are measured numerical values or counts that provide a snapshot of the application or system at a specific time. They are light and fast, with a near real-time capability. Logs contain records for all sorts of different data types captured from your telemetry, such as performance data and events.

Data can be collected from any number of sources in your environment. Azure breaks these sources down into application tiers, with your application at the top and continuing down through the operating system and internal Azure resources. Each of these tiers is broken down further into more detailed sources. For example, Azure Monitor can collect data from within the application to monitor the application and code itself through user telemetry, logs, and performance indicators. It can even collect data through a REST service, allowing for custom monitoring options that won't expose streaming data via other sources.

Azure Monitor has five categories of functions that it can perform on the metrics and logs data stores: insights, visualizations, analysis, response, and integration. These functions allow you to create dashboards, alerts, views, and much more.

There is an overview page for most Azure resources in the Azure portal that shows data collected by the monitor. For example, with the metrics explorer for a virtual machine, you can view graphs that track multiple metrics over a period of time to monitor long- or short-term performance. Or you can pin individual charts to a dashboard to provide a broad view of the information you're monitoring across your environment.

## Additional Tools Available in Azure for Monitoring

Dozens of monitoring tools made by third-party vendors are compatible with Azure. Among these, AppDynamics, Datadog, and Dynatrace also offer plug-ins for both NGINX OSS and NGINX Plus.

*AppDynamics*
> This is a full application performance–monitoring suite for monitoring enterprise applications for optimization and fine-tuning. In Azure, it has tools to monitor native services like Azure Cloud Services, virtual machines, and data storage. The AppDynamics NGINX plug-in offers additional monitoring of active connections, number of requests, accepted and handled requests, and more.

*Datadog*
> This is a popular monitoring and analytics tool in DevOps for monitoring servers, databases, and applications throughout Azure. For NGINX OSS, Datadog monitors total requests and accepted/handled/active connections. More metrics are available for NGINX Plus, such as SSL, caches, upstream server metrics, and errors.

*Dynatrace*
> Dynatrace provides monitoring for the full Azure environment without manual configuration. It uses AI for automated monitoring. NGINX integration is very robust, including network traffic analysis and retransmission metrics.

*TICK with Grafana*
> This is an open source monitoring solution. TICK stands for Telegraf, InfluxDB, Chronograf, and Kapacitor. Grafana is best known for its data visualization capabilities. Telegraf is a Python-based data collector agent used mostly for its ease of configuration, while InfluxDB is a time-series database known for its speed; Chronograf is the UI and administrative component of InfluxDB. Kapacitor is an open source data processing framework.

# Azure Security Center with NGINX

The move to cloud and hybrid solutions requires additional security practices. As its name implies, Azure Security Center is a native Azure service that provides threat prevention, detection, and response tools. There is a free tier with limited functionality and a fee-based standard tier with a complete set of security capabilities for organizations that need enhanced functionality. The free tier monitors compute, network, storage, and application resources in Azure. It also provides security policy, security assessment, security recommendations, and the ability to connect with other security partner solutions. The standard tier includes the capabilities of the free tier for on-premises environments (private cloud) plus other public clouds such as Amazon Web Services (AWS) and Google Cloud Platform (GCP). The standard tier also includes many more security features, along with the following critical security controls:

- Built-in and custom alerts
- Security event collection and advanced search
- Just-in-time virtual machine (VM) access
- Application-specific permissiveness

The NGINX configuration deployed to Azure VMs and VMSSs can have the Microsoft Monitoring Agent installed to read various security-related configurations and event logs from the VM for monitoring in Security Center. This provides a unified view of Azure resources, including NGINX resources.

## Azure Monitor with NGINX

Meaningful metrics play a crucial role in helping to understand applications and the underlying services and infrastructure they run to create nominal operational baselines and detect, investigate, and diagnose issues.

Azure Monitor integrates the capabilities of Log Analytics and Application Insights for end-to-end monitoring of applications that include NGINX as well as the VMs and VMSSs hosting NGINX.

Syslog is an event-logging protocol common to Linux and is the best way to consolidate logs from multiple sources into a single location. The Microsoft Monitoring Agent (MMA) for Linux hosting NGINX configures the local syslog daemon to forward messages to MMA, which then sends the messages to Azure Monitor, where a record is created.

## Azure Governance and Policy Management for NGINX

Azure provides a suite of tools and services to provide management to maintain applications and their supporting resources. Azure Governance is one of those tools.

Azure Governance offers the following features and services that can be implemented across all your Azure environments:

- With Azure Management Groups, you can create flexible hierarchies for applying policies across multiple subscriptions.
- Azure policies enforce different rules and effects over your resources.
- Azure Blueprints allow the creation of fully compliant environments and the ability to apply group policies to new Azure subscriptions.
- Azure Resource Graph allows fast visibility into all your resources.
- Cost Management allows the analysis of costs and the ability to monitor usage from a single dashboard.

NGINX, as well as the VMs and VMSSs hosting NGINX, can be managed with the functionality provided in Azure Governance.

# Azure Sentinel

Azure Sentinel is a managed SIEM (security information and event management) and SOAR (security orchestration, automation, and response) solution. Azure Sentinel collects all of your log and metric data and analyzes it for security incidents using machine learning. This machine learning is bootstrapped by training from years of security work done at Microsoft and further learns from your data to correlate what is normal for your application.

## Sentinel Integration

Azure Sentinel looks at all the data with which you can provide it to correlate and hunt for threats and incidents. The more data sources you provide to Sentinel, the more perspective it has. Azure Sentinel can monitor a vast array of different types of data. The simplest integrations are called *service to service* and are direct integrations:

- Amazon Web Services—CloudTrail (*https://oreil.ly/qG-Il*)
- Azure Active Directory (*https://oreil.ly/53GCc*) (audit logs and sign-in logs)
- Azure Active Directory (AD) Identity Protection (*https://oreil.ly/WSBJn*)
- Azure Activity (*https://oreil.ly/zL65e*)
- Microsoft Defender for Identity (*https://oreil.ly/ifxs5*) (formerly Azure Advanced Threat Protection)
- Azure Information Protection (*https://oreil.ly/fGxxD*)
- Azure Security Center (*https://oreil.ly/0BhWF*)
- Azure Web Application Firewall (*https://oreil.ly/sP1Az*)

- Domain name server (DNS) (*https://oreil.ly/pynGL*)
- Microsoft Cloud App Security (*https://oreil.ly/AUCaL*)
- Microsoft Defender for Endpoint (*https://oreil.ly/y8zxn*) (formerly Microsoft Defender ATP)
- Microsoft Office 365 (*https://oreil.ly/zf1M3*)
- Windows Defender Firewall with Advanced Security (*https://oreil.ly/xZkvX*)
- Windows security events (*https://oreil.ly/iUBZM*)

This set of integrations puts you in a really good place to detect threats and security incidents. Azure Sentinel can correlate events from AD with Office 365 and determine how events in those services may have been related to an Azure WAF incident.

Next, Sentinel is able to connect to a number of external solutions though their APIs. These solutions have integrated with Sentinel in such a way that Sentinel understands how to retrieve logs from the service's API. These logs are harvested and put into Azure Log Analytics where Sentinel can utilize them. Some of these external sources include:

- Alcide kAudit (*https://oreil.ly/lL_W3*)
- Barracuda CloudGen Firewall (*https://oreil.ly/UEitF*)
- Barracuda WAF (*https://oreil.ly/Icdt7*)
- Citrix Analytics (Security) (*https://oreil.ly/c4knc*)
- F5 BIG-IP (*https://oreil.ly/Gz5ZB*)
- Forcepoint DLP (*https://oreil.ly/sPsnH*)
- Perimeter 81 activity logs (*https://oreil.ly/Bpv7D*)
- Squadra Technologies secRMM (*https://oreil.ly/QM798*)
- Symantec ICDx (*https://oreil.ly/6Yx7x*)
- Zimperium Mobile Threat Defense (*https://oreil.ly/LPiK3*)

These integrations will enable Sentinel's use of common security systems that may live outside of your Azure cloud footprint. By connecting multiple solutions as data sources, we're able to bring all our security monitoring under a single pane of glass, which not only aids in our discovery but also strengthens the machine learning that's flagging events.

Other services that are not yet listed can be integrated with Sentinel through the use of an agent that acts as a syslog receiver. The logs are collected by the syslog receiver and then sent to Log Analytics, where they're made available to Sentinel. The syslog receiver converts the log stream from the common event format (CEF) and into the format needed for Log Analytics. Services that can integrate with syslog to use the Log Analytics/Sentinel agent include the following:

- Firewalls, proxies, and endpoints:
  - NGINX
  - AI Vectra Detect (*https://oreil.ly/T5O7e*)
  - Check Point (*https://oreil.ly/Wki7Q*)
  - Cisco ASA (*https://oreil.ly/hc1VG*)
  - ExtraHop Reveal(x) (*https://oreil.ly/ShHC0*)
  - F5 ASM (*https://oreil.ly/UZ9Hz*)
  - Forcepoint products (*https://oreil.ly/9QqO4*)
  - Fortinet (*https://oreil.ly/fmSha*)
  - One Identity Safeguard (*https://oreil.ly/9qqCp*)
  - Other CEF appliances (*https://oreil.ly/jGXVi*)
  - Other syslog appliances (*https://oreil.ly/0OhdU*)
  - Palo Alto Networks (*https://oreil.ly/vvRd4*)
  - Trend Micro Deep Security (*https://oreil.ly/7GmbW*)
  - Zscaler (*https://oreil.ly/tgJyi*)
- ALP solutions
- Threat intelligence providers (*https://oreil.ly/uOB0D*)
- DNS machines (*https://oreil.ly/5onOp*) (agent installed directly on the DNS machine)
- Linux servers
- Other clouds

## NGINX Sentinel integration

To integrate NGINX with the Log Analytics/Sentinel agent, you just need to turn on syslog in the NGINX configuration for the log directives:

```
error_log syslog:server={ip_of_Receiver} debug;
access_log syslog:server={ip_of_Receiver},facility=local,tag=NGX,severity=info;
```

The prior example configures NGINX to send syslog messages for errors generated by NGINX and also turns on the debug log, which provides valuable connection information when looking for security events. The example then logs all access logs to the syslog receiver, tagging them with information compliant with the common event format.

The facility attribute is meant to identify which part of the system the log came from; examples of facility names include kern (for kernel), mail, daemon, auth, and audit. The tag attribute can be any value we'd like to use; NGINX is a good identifier, but we may want to set this to be specific to a DNS name NGINX is listening for, in which case we would define our aces_log directive within a server block and use something more specific. The severity attribute is a predefined severity type; NGINX sets this to info by default. There are a number of other options, such as debug, warning, error, and critical.

More information about the syslog protocol and the CEF format can be found in the RFC 3164 (*https://oreil.ly/Q84nt*).

## Sentinel Monitoring

Sentinel Workbooks are the same as Azure Monitor Workbooks; however, they're presented differently, with security in mind. You can configure your own workbooks to enable you to view your data in any way useful to your security processes. These dashboards allow you to build detailed or high-level views of specific portions of your system while also being able to pull information from any of the data sources you've enabled.

When Sentinel detects a threat or security event, it produces analytics about that incident. An incident is reported, and data about the incident is correlated and presented to you in a concise format. Incidents are classified into severity groups: Critical, High, Medium, Low, and Informational. An incident goes through the Open, In progress, and Resolved states. This enables your security team to work from a queue of incidents that need further investigation or remediation.

## Sentinel Automation

Sentinel enables you to automatically respond to security incidents with automation through the use of playbooks. A large number of playbook integrations enable Sentinel to send messages to different systems, which may issue an alarm or take action. These integrations can also respond to the playbook so that it can further process the incident until it is resolved or sent to a human for further investigation and remediation.

A playbook is able to control the workflow as a state machine, sending notifications to managed or on-premises connectors. During the workflow, the information passed to such connectors can be manipulated with variables about the incident for basic string and object manipulation. Custom code can also be triggered to enable integration with any system or to build custom response actions by use of Azure Functions and direct inline JavaScript. You may use these abilities to integrate with third-party systems that are not prebuilt connectors or respond to incidents directly.

Sentinel provides a one-stop shop for security monitoring and response. Collecting information from all data sources possible provides Sentinel with a bird's eye view of your technology and the events that happen within it. Through the use of machine learning, Sentinel is out-of-the-box smart on security events and will automatically start to determine patterns of normal usage to spot anomalies. The incident management enables your team to stay on top of events and make sure that they've been handled. And finally, the automation abilities provide you with the capability to automatically respond to incidents, by notifying the appropriate parties, taking some action, or processing the data further. Azure Sentinel is an extremely valuable addition to any security team's tool box.

## Azure Governance and Policy Management

Azure Governance is a portion of the Azure Management area that specifically focuses on policy and cost management. Azure Governance is not a single product but rather a methodology that employs a number of Azure's features.

Governance starts by organizing your subscriptions into management groups. Management groups are logical containers of Azure subscriptions that create a hierarchy. The hierarchy enables you to apply group-wide policies that are inherited by a child from a parent. When you get started with Azure Management Groups, a root group is automatically created for you, and all subscriptions within the directory become children of the root group. Azure enforces a single hierarchy strategy to provide the administrator the ability to create top-down policies that apply to the entire directory.

### Management groups

Management groups can be divided into a hierarchy that makes sense for your organization. It's typical to see groups organized by business units, by teams, and then perhaps by project or product or environment. You can build up to 10,000 groups and have a tree that branches six levels, not including the root group.

Once you have a root group, and some hierarchy built up, you can start to apply policies to groups. Policies help to enforce standards and compliance within Azure. You can use policies to govern things like which Azure regions can be used, which SKUs can be consumed for different types of services, resource types available, and tagging.

### Policies

With policies, you provide the intent of the standard you want to enforce. Policies can be applied to audit or deny actions. When you get started with policies, resources already provisioned to a subscription will be flagged in an audit capacity as noncompliant, and remediation recommendations are provided; in addition, a remediation task is created to track the remediation effort.

Policies are different from role-based access control (RBAC). Policies do not have anything to do with the user's permissions; they're specifically about the resources being requested and ensuring that they meet the organization's standards.

When a resource is requested that does not conform to the policy, either the resource is flagged as noncompliant when the policy is in audit mode, or it is blocked from being created if the policy is set to deny. Other actions can be performed as well, such as auto-remediation, where the policy can alter the resource change request before or after the resource is provisioned.

Policies or sets of policies can be applied to management groups and subscriptions as well as to resource groups. It's suggested that you start from the topmost, broadest policy and work your way down to the lowest, most restrictive level, because of the hierarchy structure.

Any of the load balancers that you create will exist within a resource group. There can be multiple resource groups within a subscription, and multiple subscriptions within a management group. As described previously, there can be multiple management groups within an Azure directory that make up a hierarchy. Given that, at any point there may be up to three or more policies applied. The highest level takes precedence, and rules are applied from the top down within the hierarchy of management groups, subscriptions, and resource groups.

With this layered approach, administrators are able to build complex, multitiered governance over the organization's use of Azure. This control enables them to specify which regions are available for use, what type of resources can be used, and the size of those resources.

## Cost management

These concepts pair with Cost Management because they enable the ability to restrict usage for certain levels of logical resource groupings within Azure. Currently in Azure Cost Management, you can scope by management group, but you can't filter or group by management groups. Azure Billing has its own separate hierarchy that is unrelated to the management group hierarchy. This makes sense when you consider that the management side of things does not always map one-to-one with the accounting side of the organization.

One way to aggregate costs is through the use of tags, which, as you may remember, is one of the resource attributes you can govern with policies. At your root management group layer, you can enforce a policy that requires specific tags to be set for billing aggregation. Within a child management group layer, you may default the tag to a value, and so on down the hierarchy. Tag policies and defaults can be set at any layer; it simply makes sense that sublevels are where things would be defaulted.

## Example scenario

As an example, let's examine an Azure VM running NGINX as our resource request. The NGINX VM must exist within a resource group, within a subscription. The subscription is logically grouped under a management group named Sandbox. The sandbox management group is a child of the App-Dev management group, which is a child of the root management group. Figure 6-1 shows this hierarchy in a diagram.

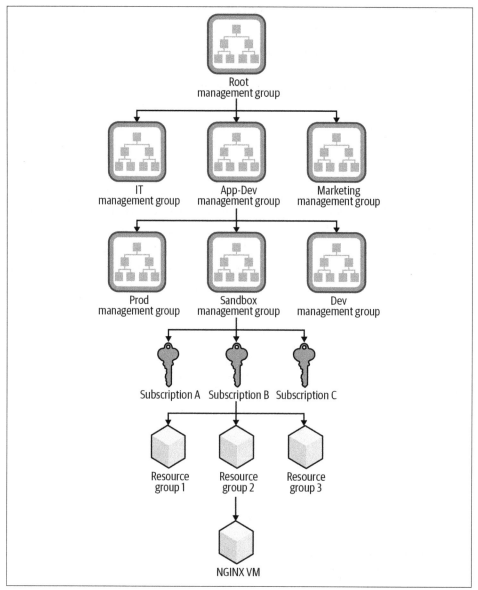

*Figure 6-1. Example of governance hierarchy.*

At the root layer, we may apply a policy that all resources must be tagged with the following tags:

- Business Unit
- Environment
- Application
- Service

In our child management group, Sandbox, we can enforce all of these tags as well but default or require the Business Unit tag to be set to "App-Dev." In the child management group of the App-Dev management group, we can default or require the Environment tag to be set to a value of "Sandbox." The subscription may have a policy, though it also may not enforce any tagging standards or defaults. Applying a policy to the resource group may default or require the Application tag to be set to the name of the application or service offering. At this point, the only tag that is not set by default is the Service tag. This means that when we create our NGINX VM, we must specify that a tag named Service is set to a value.

When we create the NGINX VM, specifying that the Service tag be set to a value of "NGINX," our VM will be created and automatically tagged as follows:

- Business Unit: App-Dev
- Environment: Sandbox
- Application: Ecommerce
- Service: NGINX

With this layer of governance, we're able to ensure that accounting is able to aggregate costs down to the service level of an application within any environment for any business unit.

Furthermore, we're able to control what size of VM is used for NGINX by specifying policies that restrict SKUs. For example, let's say that marketing requires various types of large instances for machine learning, and we do not wish to cap the SKU usage for VMs at the root level. We can specify that the App-Dev business unit's Sandbox management group must run only Standard-level VMs but that the production environment must be able to use certain specialized SKU types.

We would apply a policy to the Sandbox management unit that specifies that only Standard SKU VMs are allowed to be created. This enables us to manage spend by not allowing our development team to utilize overly provisioned machines for testing.

With geological/regional controls, we're able to define where the virtual machine is created. The other feature of policies allows us to specify which services are available for use—for example, enabling directory services in the IT management group but not in other groups.

With these controls, you're able, through a hierarchy, to govern what gets created where in your Azure environment without having to consider who is requesting the resource, enabling a high-to-low-level control interface over your environment.

## Conclusion

This chapter covered general information about Azure governance, monitoring, and security. This information provides you with multiple options for controlling your Azure subscription hierarchy, in which your load balancers live, and for monitoring your load-balancing solutions at multiple layers, including security.

In the final chapter, we will take a closer look at security in the context of NGINX and Azure Firewall.

# CHAPTER 7

# Security

Security is everyone's job. To maintain a secure system, you need as many layers of controls as possible. Azure and NGINX offer a number of those layers for the data plane. These layers come as features of control and visibility. Managed Azure services integrate directly with Azure Monitor. Third-party data plane services, such as NGINX, can integrate with Azure Monitor, as well as through the use of an agent. Third-party services such as NGINX sometimes offer their own monitoring capabilities as well.

The previous chapter focused on monitoring; the amount of information you can gather from monitoring the data plane is vast. The data plane sees every request to and within your web application. With what you learned in the monitoring chapter, you now have visibility into those requests. With a public web application, you may see metric values that surprise you—perhaps your application is popular with bots, for instance. A look into the access logs, which show what requests are getting made, may have scared you. It's common for bots and hackers to scan an endpoint for known vulnerabilities.

There's a lot at stake for a web application. In the obvious cases, sensitive data must not be leaked or breached. It's our understanding that the Capital One data breach was spawned from a Server-Side Request Forgery (SSRF) attack, a type of attack that is well-known and covered by the OWASP Core Rule Set. It was not that Capital One was not using a WAF; they were—ModSecurity, in fact. It was that the applied Mod-Security rules were misconfigured, allowing the attacker to run commands on the server to return access credentials with more privilege than they should have had. Once the attacker had the credentials, they were able to retrieve the data of 160 million people.

After seeing the type of requests your application is receiving, and knowing that simple misconfiguration can cause such massive damage, you're ready to do something about it and protect your application. Securing a web application requires controls around management, accurate detection of issues through audits and monitoring, and active prevention. This chapter will focus on security controls and visibility of those controls for audits and active monitoring use of NGINX and Azure products.

# NGINX Management with NGINX Controller

NGINX Controller is an application-centric control plane for your application environments. Controller provides a web-based user interface and API for interacting with a fleet of NGINX Plus servers. Controller elevates your data plane from a low-level NGINX Plus file-based configuration to a higher-level configuration with respect to the applications themselves. You tell Controller about your applications and how you want them presented, and Controller handles the NGINX Plus configuration and distribution of that configuration to the NGINX Plus nodes. Controller is a commercial product available from NGINX, Inc., as an add-on to an NGINX Plus environment.

Figure 7-1 shows the NGINX Controller platform, depicting the type of users that may interface with it, the available ecosystem integrations, and the controlled layers between the application code and the user.

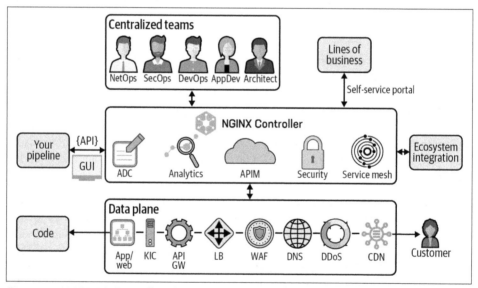

*Figure 7-1. NGINX Controller platform.*

Controller is infrastructure and cloud agnostic, which means you can use it to manage NGINX Plus nodes wherever they may be. This is extremely useful for multicloud or hybrid cloud deployments.

When using NGINX Controller, you have a single interface to control and monitor your NGINX Plus fleet. Controller provides different views that pertain to specific sections of the stack. The platform view is used for managing NGINX Controller settings and user access. Users can be granted access only to specific views that pertain to their role within an organization; this enables a self-service model. The infrastructure view details information about the NGINX Plus nodes running the Controller agent. The services view organizes and manages objects pertaining to applications, environments, gateways, and APIs. The analytics view provides access to metric information about services and NGINX Plus instances.

The applications, environments, gateways, and APIs are the application-centric configuration objects that make up how NGINX Controller delivers your applications. An application represents your web application, which is further broken into components describing how to reach the services-offering portions of your application.

The end user–facing side of an application is defined at the gateway, which represents an NGINX Plus node server configuration. An environment gives you the ability to group and isolate configurations and access to resources across stages such as test and production. This is a powerful way to take a single configuration and advance it through stages until release. APIs provide the ability to tightly define specific API configurations when NGINX Plus is acting as an API gateway or service mesh.

By splitting management and usage, Controller provides teams with an integration point. It also applies a layer of safety for your teams as they share physical resources. Infrastructure teams make servers available by connecting NGINX Plus nodes to Controller. Security teams make TLS certificates available and have a single pane of glass for data plane security controls and security events. Developers and Operations teams can utilize these resources to focus on their application delivery with all these other components abstracted.

NGINX Controller fits directly into an application code deployment pipeline by centralizing NGINX Plus management into a single system. The NGINX Controller configuration is driven by an API that is available to its users. Each entity or configuration object in Controller can be managed through this API; when using the UI, each create or update action to an entity shows the exact API call that can be used to perform the same action in an automated fashion. An NGINX-maintained Ansible collection helps teams using Ansible configuration management to integrate directly with the Controller API.

 Ansible is a configuration management tool that defines the desired state of system configuration through declarative configuration. It can be used to automate bootstrapping and ongoing configuration updates of a virtual machine.

# NGINX Controller Application Delivery Module with App Security Add-On

Centralizing control and monitoring of your data plane makes it easy to manage, audit the current security state, and get visibility on security incidents as well. NGINX Controller Application Delivery Module with App Security enables the use of a Web Application Firewall to protect apps from web-based threats. The App Security Add-On controls the NGINX App Protect module that runs on top of NGINX Plus, serving as the WAF enforcement point on the data plane that sits in front of the application. WAF can be enabled via NGINX Controller by adding a few more parameters to the specification for enabling traffic management services via an NGINX Controller API endpoint or the web-based user interface. It also collects WAF information from the data plane to provide loopback and threat visibility (how many violations and what violations) from WAF.

Figure 7-2 shows an example of a graph provided by NGINX Controller Application Delivery Module with App Security Add-On that compares normal traffic and suspicious or blocked traffic trends over time.

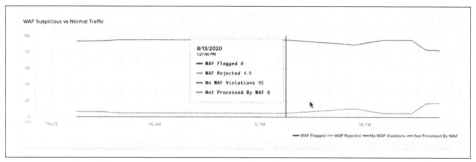

*Figure 7-2. Controller ADC comparing normal traffic versus suspicious or blocked traffic.*

This optional and separate NGINX product is fully functional within Azure and provides an additional or exclusive way to manage NGINX without the use of Azure Security Center, Azure Monitor, or Azure Portal or PowerShell. Figure 7-3 depicts an administrator's control of the data plane using high-level concepts provided by Controller.

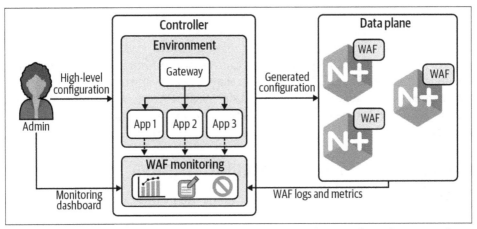

*Figure 7-3. Administration with high-level concepts to configure a fleet of NGINX Plus servers with WAF capabilities.*

## NGINX App Protect

As mentioned in "Comparing NGINX and Azure Web Application Firewall Capabilities" on page 60, you can add WAF to NGINX Plus without using NGINX Controller. NGINX App Protect is built on F5's WAF and bot protection, runs natively on NGINX Plus, and integrates security controls into your application.

# NGINX ModSecurity WAF

Also mentioned in "Comparing NGINX and Azure Web Application Firewall Capabilities" on page 60, NGINX can use ModSecurity directly to act as a Web Application Firewall. To use ModSecurity, you need to build and install the ModSecurity project as well as the NGINX module. NGINX's "Compiling and Installing ModSecurity for NGINX Open Source" (*https://oreil.ly/uC1H_*) guide is extremely useful when going through this process.

To those using NGINX Plus, NGINX, Inc., offers an additional product, NGINX ModSecurity WAF. This product includes a ModSecurity module built, tested, and supported by NGINX, Inc. This product is an add-on to an NGINX Plus subscription.

An open source security scanning tool called Nikto can be used to test the WAF rules. Nikto scans an HTTP endpoint for known common security vulnerabilities and will demonstrate that the ModSecurity rules are working.

An important part of security is control. When managing a fleet of NGINX servers, their configuration should be under management through a configuration management tool. Configuration management tools enable keeping configuration as code in source control. With configuration management, you can enforce the use of these rules on your NGINX configuration. To ensure that the enforcement does not get turned off, many source control systems have a feature called code owners. This enables the source control repository to require approval from certain users or teams for updates to specific files. It's possible to require approval from security personnel for changes to base templates that enable the WAF settings, for example. We bring this up because this type of integration between teams lessens the burden of change management.

# Microsoft Azure Firewall Integration into a Load-Balancing Solution

Azure Firewall is a managed, cloud-based network security service that protects your Azure Virtual Network resources. It is a fully stateful Firewall-as-a-Service with built-in high availability and unrestricted cloud scalability. You can centrally create, enforce, and log application and network connectivity policies across subscriptions and virtual networks.

Azure Firewall is a regional service that spans availability zones. Azure Firewall works like a traditional network firewall but is fully managed. You can add NAT, network, and application rules, grouped as collections. Azure Firewall filters in and out of Azure Virtual Network.

To integrate with a load-balancing solution, you would configure inbound DNAT support. This feature enables you to run a traditional firewall in front of your load-balancing device. Your rule would simply specify the source address as the network you want to allow traffic from. The destination address would be the public IP of the Firewall, and the port value would be set to the port in which your application receives traffic from the public. The translated address and port values tell the Azure Firewall where to direct the traffic if it's allowed; this is where you would enter your load balancer information. This may be an NGINX virtual machine, or it may be an Azure Load Balancer that is load balancing for specific services or for NGINX acting as an API gateway.

Once configured, your traffic should be directed to the Azure Firewall public IP address. The Azure Firewall will filter inbound traffic to your load balancer for only network communication approved by the rule groups.

The Azure Firewall can also work as an outbound NAT that receives traffic from within the Virtual Network and filters outbound communication for only known allowed traffic. It can even be directed to send outbound traffic to a specific next hop, such as another firewall either on-premises or on a virtual machine within Azure. Outbound filtering can be done with FQDNs as well as network rules and does not interrupt a TLS connection.

The threat intelligence feature applies the Microsoft Threat Intelligence feed to your Firewall rules. Threat Intelligence is a feed of security signatures produced by years of research and machine learning on Microsoft's global view of the internet's threat landscape. This feature keeps your firewall up to date to block and alert for traffic going to or coming from known malicious IPs and domain names.

The Azure Firewall is a nice security bonus in the Azure cloud. Its integration with Azure Monitor and Azure Firewall Manager makes analytics, monitoring, and management native.

# NGINX Integration as an NVA Firewall

NVA, or network virtual appliance, is the name for a pattern in which a virtual machine performs networking functions. It is usually isolated in its own virtual network segment and is the main entry point to and/or from the internet. To utilize NGINX as a Layer 7 NVA, you would construct a subnet within your virtual network and label it something like "Public DMZ," for "demilitarized zone." Your NGINX nodes would go in this subnet.

A separate subnet for your application servers would also be built. Routing to the application or private subnet is possible only through internal route tables for the virtual network. This means that these servers are not accessible from the public internet. Requests must be routed through your DMZ and your NVA before being passed to your application. This gives NGINX the position of sitting between public traffic and your applications. Figure 7-4 depicts the network and infrastructure when using an NVA inline between the public internet and your applications.

You can use a public Azure Load Balancer to balance traffic over highly available NGINX nodes. The NGINX nodes would filter traffic based on the Load Balancer's own rules, such as allowed networks, request valuation, and WAF rules.

NGINX would not be used for outbound filtering; for an outbound Layer 7 NVA, you could use something like Squid to provide an outbound HTTP(S) proxy.

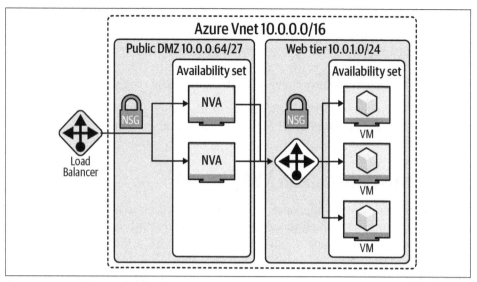

*Figure 7-4. Highly available Layer 7 ingress NVA firewalls in front of a set of servers.*

# Conclusion

Throughout this book, you've learned a lot about application delivery and load balancing. Our hope is that you now understand that there are different layers of proxies and load balancers that can provide functionality at varying levels of the stack. With this information, you can deliver your application at a global scale with features that enable resiliency, performance, and security.

Azure managed services provide a lot of functionality out of the box. Our advice to you is to always opt for managed services until your need outgrows their functionality. Managed services will always be cheaper when evaluated for total cost of ownership. The amount of cost, capital and opportunistic, that is saved by not sinking engineering time and management into maintaining your own solution allows your team to focus on its core objective: the application.

When the needs of advanced features do outgrow managed services, there are application delivery platforms and load balancers that can take your Layer 7 traffic routing to the next level. NGINX and NGINX Plus have a lot of overlapping features that you might also find in Azure managed services; however, they can be used in conjunction with each other when operating at different levels—Front Door before NGINX as an API gateway, for example. NGINX provides advanced controls when necessary but still has all the core features necessary for building out a reliable, performant, and secure data plane.

The data plane is an optimal place to have good monitoring, as it sees every request entering your system, as well as between services. This layer of your web stack produces metrics and logs vital to understanding the overall health of your system. Knowing who sent a request for what, to where, and when provides you all the information you need to tune and secure effectively. With the information you learned in this book, you're on your way to delivering meaningful information from your system to your monitoring platform.

Resources like the Azure Firewall and NGINX put themselves at the edge to provide a first-layer defense against attacks. Products like NGINX Controller or configuration management tools centralize configuration to enable teams to efficiently manage and audit configuration. Monitoring integrations provide feedback on the current state of communication and active security events. These abilities combine to enable teams to be in tune with their application security.

We hope you found this book useful and applicable to your web application footprint. Go forth and use your new knowledge.

# Index

# About the Authors

**Derek DeJonghe** has had a lifelong passion for technology. His background and experience in web development, system administration, and networking give him a well-rounded understanding of modern web architecture. Derek leads a team of site reliability and cloud solution engineers and produces self-healing, autoscaling infrastructure for numerous applications. He specializes in Linux cloud environments. While designing, building, and maintaining highly available applications for clients, he consults for larger organizations as they embark on their journey to the cloud. Derek and his team are on the forefront of a technology tidal wave and are engineering cloud best practices every day. With a proven track record for resilient cloud architecture, Derek pioneers cloud deployments for security and maintainability in the best interest of his clients.

**Arlan Nugara** is a cloud solution architect who speaks widely on Azure and DevOps. Microsoft has awarded him an MVP (Most Valuable Professional) in Azure for the past two years for his expertise and contributions to the technical community across the United States and Canada. Arlan's original background is in software development with a specialization in enterprise software development and architecture for financial institutions over the previous 20 years. Arlan's focus over the past two years has been the building of Azure Virtual Datacenters, where security is a key driving factor for a client's migration to the Azure cloud. A critical part of this approach is the building of a landing zone as a configured environment with a standard set of secured cloud infrastructure, policies, best practices, guidelines, and centrally managed services.

## Colophon

The animal on the cover of *Application Delivery and Load Balancing in Microsoft Azure* is a blue-bearded bee eater (*Nyctyornis athertoni*). This bird is found in a variety of habitats across the Indian subcontinent and parts of Southeast Asia. As its name suggests, it feeds primarily on bees.

The blue-bearded bee eater has a long sick-shaped bill, a green body with a turquoise head and chin, and a yellowish breast and belly with streaks of green or blue. Its elongated throat feathers are often fluffed out, giving the bird its 'bearded' moniker. The bird's overall coloration changes depending on its region, with the birds in peninsular India having slightly lighter green body coloration, for example. Male and female blue-bearded bee-eaters look similar for the most part, although the male's blue throat-feathers tend to have higher ultraviolet reflectivity.

The call of this bird is loud and has some variation, but is relatively infrequent; they are not as vocal or active as other bee-eater species. Pairs of these birds, however, may engage in chatter that culminates in a kind of purring. The mating rituals of these birds include feeding, bowing, and tail fanning. Their nests are deep tunnels in mud banks, and the eggs they lay are white and spherical. While the blue-bearded bee-eater has been observed around various flower species, it's unclear whether they feed on the nectar or the insects it attracts.

Although challenging to spot in the wild in some regions, the conservation status of this species is "Least Concern." Many of the animals on O'Reilly covers are endangered; all of them are important to the world.

The cover illustration is by Karen Montgomery, based on a black and white engraving from Lydekker's *Royal Natural History*. The cover fonts are Gilroy Semibold and Guardian Sans. The text font is Adobe Minion Pro; the heading font is Adobe Myriad Condensed; and the code font is Dalton Maag's Ubuntu Mono.

# O'REILLY®

# There's much more where this came from.

Experience books, videos, live online training courses, and more from O'Reilly and our 200+ partners—all in one place.

Learn more at oreilly.com/online-learning

Lightning Source UK Ltd.
Milton Keynes UK
UKHW031519201220
375298UK00005B/10